# Week-by-Week

# VEGETABLE GARDENER'S

# Handbook

# Week-by-Week

# VEGETABLE

# GARDENER'S

# Handbook

### Perfectly Timed Gardening
### for Your Most Bountiful Harvest Ever

**RON KUJAWSKI**
**&**
**JENNIFER KUJAWSKI**

Storey Publishing

*The mission of Storey Publishing is to serve our customers by
publishing practical information that encourages
personal independence in harmony with the environment.*

Edited by Carleen Madigan
Art direction and book design by Cynthia N. McFarland
Cover design by Alethea Morrison
Text production by Liseann Karandisecky

Back cover illustration by © Elayne Sears
Interior illustrations by © Elayne Sears, except for pages 46 and 164 by Beverly Duncan, and pages 14, 28, 41, 45,
    55, 69, 88, 92, 109, 119, 130 right, 131 bottom, 143 top, and 176 by Judy Eliason.
Decorative illustrations by © iStockphoto.com

Indexed by Nancy D. Wood

**Storey Publishing**
210 MASS MoCA Way
North Adams, MA 01247
*www.storey.com*

Printed in China by R.R. Donnelley
10  9  8  7  6  5  4  3  2

**Library of Congress Cataloging-in-Publication Data**

Kujawski, Ron.
    The week-by-week vegetable gardener's handbook / by Ron Kujawski and Jennifer Kujawski.
        p. cm.
    Includes index.
    ISBN 978-1-60342-694-7 (paper w/partially concealed wire-o : alk. paper)
    1. Vegetable gardening. I. Kujawski, Jennifer. II. Title.
SB321.K85 2011
635—dc22
                            2010029512

Farmers Almanac
April 17
Avg. last frost
date.

Oct. 16
Avg. 1st frost
date

# Contents

NOAA
May 9

*This book is dedicated to the memory of Pauline and Andrew Kujawski.*

*Their love of the land, commitment to growing and preserving their own food,*

*and farming skills inspired us to become vegetable gardeners.*

# Acknowledgments

Our sincere thanks to all who have made this book possible. We're especially grateful to our editor, Carleen Madigan, who astutely guided our progress, often while bravely sampling our culinary experiments. She tolerated our many questions and quirky sense of humor with patience and a smile. Thanks also go to the effusive Susan Young, for her positive critique of our first draft; former colleague John Howell, retired UMass Extension vegetable specialist, for his advice and willingness to fact-check; and Randall Prostak, for taking fantastic promotional photos while keeping us in stitches with his endless store of bad jokes.

While we supplied the words, the talented folks at Storey Publishing worked their magic to make the pages jump to life. We are grateful to art director Cindy McFarland, designer Liseann Karandisecky, creative director Alethea Morrison, illustration coordinator Ilona Sherratt, and illustrator Elayne Sears.

Finally, we could not have done this without the encouragement and support of our family. To Pat (wife and mom), for endless cups of hot tea, snacks, unlimited babysitting, and occasional proofreading and refereeing our "spirited" debates; and to Bill and Liam, for their good-natured acceptance of an absentee wife and mom while we wrote this book.

# Introduction

AFTER A CUP or two of java to shake off the effects of the previous evening's revelry, many people begin the New Year by making resolutions. These are usually very personal decisions: lose weight, get more exercise, and be nicer to grumpy Aunt Tilly. We don't want to butt in on such private matters . . . well, yes we do. We suggest another resolution: Start a vegetable garden or improve on the one you already have. The fact that you're reading this is a good sign that you may have made that commitment.

There's nothing unusual about making resolutions. What's less common is actually seeing those resolutions through to a successful outcome. We believe the key to success is having a plan.

We wrote this book to help both beginning gardeners and experienced ones by taking readers through a week-by-week plan for the growing season. Just what the "growing season" is depends on where you live and your climate. The timing of gardening activities is largely determined by temperatures, specifically *low* temperatures. Rather than a one-size-fits-all approach, we base the week-by-week plan on the average date of last frost, which differs according to where you garden.

The techniques we describe and observations we make represent our approach. Experienced gardeners might have different ways of growing specific crops, but they'll find some of our methods worth a try. It may be comforting to know that the two of us don't always agree and will often argue about the best way to go about growing certain vegetables. Lively exchanges are part of the fun of gardening — so share thoughts and ideas, and be willing to explore other techniques and crops. After all, there is more than one way to skin a cat (not that we are encouraging such behavior). Over time, you will adjust how you garden to suit your particular circumstances. You may even find that

your ways are better than ours. Don't worry; we won't feel bad if you do.

This book is meant to be more than a guide to vegetable gardening; it is also intended to be a workbook. It should not remain in pristine condition. Avid gardeners have our permission — indeed our blessing — to scribble notes, make adjustments in the timing of activities based on local conditions, revise some methods to fit their preferred practices, and add their own opinions. If, after the first growing season, this book has no soil smudges or pencil marks, you probably didn't have enough fun.

Getting started in vegetable gardening is often a matter of overcoming inertia. For that reason, we have tried to make this book as simple as possible. We've given preference to breadth and brevity, rather than to depth of information. We want to help you get started and see the season through for many different crops, but our emphasis is on the more popular vegetables. There are many superb books on vegetable gardening that go into far more detail (see Resources, page 185, for a few of our favorites). Volumes can be added to your bookshelf as your interest grows and you become more confident in your gardening skills. We do cover a few subjects in greater depth, but hopefully not deep enough to drown you in minutiae.

"If you have a garden and a library, you have everything you need."

— Cicero

# Getting STARTED

AS WE MENTIONED in the introduction, getting started is often a matter of overcoming inertia. To do this, *think small.* That concept may not make it in the corporate world, but it makes sense for many gardeners. Perhaps the most common mistake novice and — we hate to admit it — even experienced gardeners make is to let the juices of early-spring enthusiasm overcome rational thought. To this day, we bite off more than we can chew and often find ourselves over-extended with a garden so large we get the feeling that we're in the middle of a Nebraska corn-field. Keeping up with such a vast enterprise is discouraging and is bound to dampen the spirits of the beginning gardener who has yet to exult in the satisfaction of a successful harvest.

*A small raised bed is all you need to grow a few tomato plants, bush beans, basil, leaf lettuce, and bush-type summer squash.*

## Small Is Good

Therefore, think small. Plan your first garden to include just a few favorite vegetables, no more than can be eaten fresh. Save those dreams about preserving huge surpluses of vegetables for winter consumption until you are comfortable with home growing.

What is small? It could be a garden that consists of just a few vegetables grown in containers on a deck or patio. It could also be a 3-by-6-foot raised bed built from landscape timbers or 2-by-8 boards.

### Use Your Hands

We often suggest that first-time gardeners turn over soil for a new garden by hand, using a garden spade or fork. The point at which they become too weary to continue is when they have the right-size garden for their first effort. Nowadays, with tillers making light duty of soil prepa-ration, first-timers often give in to the tendency to try to plow up the south forty. Resist that temp-tation, because when the weather gets hot and humid in midsum-mer, your thoughts may drift to activities more leisurely than weeding.

### Grow What You Eat

The size of the garden is determined in part by the vegetables you want to grow and perhaps by the amount of suitable space. When we get together to plan our garden and order seeds, the first consideration is, "What do family members like to eat?" (In our family, we have few beet fans. If planted at all, it will be a short row, a very short row, for the beet. One of us is an heirloom-variety enthusiast, but we grow very limited amounts of heirloom vegetables until they prove themselves.) Experience will eventually dictate what crops and how much of each to grow, but initially think small (sensing a theme here?). Seed packets of some vegetables contain enough seed to feed the armies of several small countries if all were planted at once. *You don't have to sow every seed.*

**Prioritize your planting.** Also, keep in mind the amount of space required by specific crops. In a small garden, a few pumpkin or winter squash plants can take up most of the space. So give priority to vegetables that provide continuous yield and produce the highest yields for the space allotted. These include tomatoes, beans, bush-type summer squash, peppers, and leafy greens. (See Getting More from Less: Space-Saving Gardening, page 12, for more details.)

### Location, Location, Location

Site selection is also critical when planning the garden. Just about all vegetable crops grow best in full sun. What is full sun? It is most often described as a minimum of 6 hours of direct sunlight illuminating the garden. However, we prefer to add several hours to that definition to ensure the best results.

**Ditch the swamp.** Drainage is also a key consideration when deciding where to locate your garden. Swampland will not do. Vegetable crops require good drainage — that is, water must not accumulate or puddle in the garden for long periods of time. Roots of

*Sprawling vines of pumpkin or winter squash quickly use up space in a small garden plot. Better choices for small gardens are vegetables that produce lots of food throughout the growing season.*

vegetable crops will die in soils that remain waterlogged for more than a few days. Poorly drained sites are ones that are in depressions or have soil with high clay content. Avoid planting in these sites, if possible. However, if you have no choice, building raised beds on the site will allow you to grow vegetables. Although that will add to the initial expense of making a garden, it will give you fewer headaches in the long run.

**Dealing with dry soil.** At the other end of the drainage spectrum are soils that drain too quickly. This is a problem for those who garden in soils that are very sandy or gravelly. It's not surprising that vegetation of any sort is rather sparse on such soils — picture a desert or seashore. Since vegetable crops need ample amounts of water for good growth and abundant yields, it's quite a challenge for gardeners with the misfortune of living in what basically amounts to a desert.

That's not to say that it's impossible to grow crops on such sites. It can be done. The big question for gardeners with fast-draining soils is, "How do I get my soil to hold moisture?" There are a couple of ways to do this. One is to add lots of organic matter to the soil. Organic matter acts like a sponge to absorb and hold water. Reducing evaporation is another option. Applying mulches — preferably organic mulch such as straw, salt-marsh

hay, chopped leaves, grass clippings, or compost — to the soil surface will reduce evaporation. Since wind speeds the evaporation of moisture from soils, setting up some type of windbreak will slow evaporation. A windbreak can be a fence, a building, or a planting of trees on the windward side of the garden. If you plant trees, put them far enough away from the garden that the tree roots do not compete with the roots of vegetable plants for soil moisture.

**Siting for convenience.** Having said all that, we know that locating a garden for convenience is just as important a consideration: putting the garden in some far-off corner where you have to cart tools and drag hoses and watering cans is not a recipe for success. If the garden is near the house (or a well-traveled area), near a water source, and near your tools, you will be more likely to spend time in it caring for plants and noticing the little things: developing fruits and vegetables or emerging pests, diseases, and weeds.

---

## GROWING IN PARTIAL SUN

Some vegetable crops can do very well in less than full sun. Here's the Gardener's Guide to Growing in Gloomy Gardens:

- In gardens receiving 5 to 6 hours of direct sunlight, plant beets, carrots, onions, kohlrabi, turnips, tomatoes, peppers, beans, squash, and herbs such as cilantro, dill, thyme, and sweet marjoram. These root crops and fruiting crops give the highest yields and tastiest harvest when grown in full sun.

- In areas with 2 to 4 hours of sun, plant leafy greens and scallions, as well as parsley, chives, and basil. In fact, leafy greens will appreciate receiving only morning sun during the hottest part of the summer.

- Shady gardens receiving only dappled sunlight can be planted with endive, leeks, leaf lettuce, spinach, radishes, turnip greens, and small-headed varieties of cabbage.

- If the garden is in heavy shade (similar to the deep woods), you'd best plant yourself in line at the local produce market.

## Getting More from Less: Space-Saving Gardening

"I don't have the space to plant a vegetable garden." For some, that's a convenient excuse to avoid gardening. Unfortunately, for too many people it is a reality. Yet there are ways of growing at least a few vegetables when space is at a premium. Even those gardeners with a good amount of space can get more from it by employing a few of the following strategies.

### Best Bets for Small Spots

The first step is to select crops that are space efficient. These are vegetables that have high yields and that continue to produce a harvest through much of the growing season. Among these we include tomatoes, peppers, bush beans, pole beans, cucumbers, carrots, summer squash, and most greens, such as leaf lettuce, chard, and kale. These greens are often called "cut-and-come-again" crops because they can be harvested by cutting off the leaves (*outer* leaves for the chard and kale). With their centers (called crowns) intact, the plants will continue to produce more leaves for continuous harvest.

Crops that we suggest avoiding if space is very limited are sweet corn and most vine crops, such as pumpkins, winter squash, and melons. However, some newer varieties of vine crops have actually been bred to save space.

Certain winter squash, melons, and cucumbers that once grew only as long vines are now available in bush form. Some of these are:

*Cucumber: Bush Champion, Bush Pickle, Salad Bush, Spacemaster*

*Muskmelon: Minnesota Midget, Honey Bun Hybrid*

*Winter squash: Bush Delicata, Table Ace*

Search your seed catalogs for others, as new ones appear each year. We'll have to admit that some of the varieties we tried were not worth the effort, as the fruits were small and the plants did not always have a high yield. At least that's been our experience in the past; you may be more successful!

### Growing Up

Space can also be used more efficiently by going, or should we say "growing," vertical. Vine crops (cucumbers, pole beans, squash, tall peas, tomatoes) can be grown on trellises or fences to save garden space. Some vine crops may even be grown in hanging baskets or grow-bags and allowed to drape down. Besides saving space, hanging baskets offer the additional advantage of being out of reach of ground-dwelling pests like slugs.

## Well-Planned Planting

Like many gardeners out there, we'd rather be planting than planning. But getting the most out of a garden takes preparation. Below are several planting schemes that can make your planning easier. We've used these plans successfully to increase our garden's productivity.

### Succeeding with Succession

Crop succession is one scheme that makes a great deal of sense. One method of succession planting involves sowing multiple crops of a vegetable that has a short growing season. In other words, after you harvest early-

*Use garden space more efficiently by growing vine crops such as cucumbers on a trellis.*

planted radishes or spinach, make another planting of the same vegetable in that space. Crop succession could also be done by sequencing early-, midseason, and late-season crops in the same garden space. As an example of such a sequence, plant radish or leaf lettuce as the early-season crop, follow its harvest with a planting of summer squash for the midseason or summer crop, and then plant greens or root crops for late-season harvest in the same location.

### Mix It Up

Intercropping is another planting scheme to make efficient use of space. This method involves planting fast-growing vegetables among slow growers. Radishes and carrots sown in the same row is a common example. The radish seedlings come up first, and by the time they are harvested, the carrots are ready to expand into space formerly occupied by the radishes. Intercropping can also be done by alternating rows of fast-growing vegetables with slow growers. The fast grower completes its growth cycle at the time the slow grower needs space to expand into. We've planted rows of lettuce between rows of tomato plants, for example.

### Wide Rows and Square Feet

Wide-row planting and its many variations, such as square-foot gardening and block planting, are popular ways to grow more in less space. With these planting schemes, the normal spacing recommendations for seeding are ignored and crops are planted by randomly scattering seeds over a wide row of 18 to 24 inches and then thinning crowded seedlings. This works especially well when growing crops in raised beds.

As a variation on wide-row planting, we frequently employ double rowing for many crops. For example, we transplant individual onion seedlings at the recommended spacing of 3 to 4 inches in a row. Traditionally, the next row is spaced 16 inches from the first. However, we plant our second row only 4 inches from the first. This is our double row. We plant subsequent sets of double rows 16 inches away from

*Planting in double rows or staggered triple rows is a great way to save valuable garden space.*

the set before it. (This is one case where a picture is worth a thousand words — see the illustration of double rowing on page 13.) Double rowing works well for just about all crops except vine crops. We carry this idea one step further when planting cabbage, broccoli, and cauliflower seedlings. The normal in-row spacing for these is about 18 inches between plants, so we plant three staggered rows with plants all 18 inches apart in the rows and between the rows.

### Season Extending = Maximizing Harvest

Some of the strategies for getting more from less space are the same as those for extending the season. These include starting the season early by planting cold-tolerant vegetables, starting certain vegetables indoors so that they can be transplanted to spaces vacated by early-season crops, using raised beds and other soil-warming techniques, and employing cold-protection devices such as cold frames.

### Raised Beds

Raised beds offer opportunities to save space because you can put a small raised bed just about anywhere. The beds could be any shape: they could be square, rectangular, or even triangular if necessary to fit into a corner of the yard. However, the real space saving with raised beds comes from the fact that the deep, loose soil facilitates deep root development, which means that vegetables can be planted much closer together than they would be in the garden.

### Crops in Pots

Where no usable garden space exists, grow vegetables in containers. Even where space for a garden exists, you'll find some advantages to growing certain vegetables in containers. Plants often grow better in containers because they are easier to maintain on a regular basis and because they are growing in

*Many vegetables and fruits — like strawberries, tomatoes, herbs, and lettuce — are well suited to growing in containers.*

*Use less soil in a large container by (a) filling the container two-thirds full with shredded leaves, (b) putting soil over the top of leaves, and (c) adding more soil to fill container after the leaves have settled.*

ideal soil. Soil for containers is made by combining organic matter, such as screened compost or peat moss, with coarse sand, vermiculite, or perlite. This soil typically has better texture and more nutrient- and water-holding ability than garden soils do.

One of the common complaints about growing vegetables in large and deep containers is the volume of soil needed to fill the containers. Here's a little trick we've used very successfully. Fill your empty container two-thirds full with shredded leaves saved from fall raking, then place your soil mix on top of the leaves. Expect some immediate settling, after which you may incorporate additional soil. By doing this, you'll need to use only about half the amount of soil that would otherwise be needed. Some more settling will occur as the season progresses and the leaves decompose, but this isn't a problem. At the end of the season, you'll find a nice layer of decayed leaves at the bottom of each pot, which you can dump onto your garden. It's a good way to add organic matter to your garden soil.

Containers used to grow vegetables can be anything from large clay or plastic pots to wooden barrels, patio pots, bushel baskets, or an old shoe, size 12 or larger. The only restrictions on containers are that they have drainage holes and have not previously held any toxic substances.

Over the years, we've experimented with growing just about every vegetable in a container, including sweet corn and potatoes. While all have done well, the high-yield, continuous-harvest vegetables (tomato, pepper, bush and pole beans, cucumber, and summer squash) make the most sense for container growing.

Vegetable plants in containers require more attention than do those in a garden. Container-grown crops need to be watered daily, sometimes even twice daily, as the small volume of soil tends to dry quickly in hot weather. Because of frequent watering, plant nutrients will leach from the soil. Leaching is less likely with slow-release natural fertilizers. That's why we prefer to incorporate this type of fertilizer into the container soil prior to planting.

For anyone who complains about not having room to grow vegetables, space is the next frontier.

# FROM THE
# Ground Up

"DON'T PUT a ten-dollar plant in a one-dollar hole." Though there are many versions of that old saying, the point is the same: good soil preparation is a key to successful gardening. Garden soil provides roots with the nutrients necessary for plant growth and at its best is fluffy, weed-free, and full of air pockets. It is rich in organic matter and holds moisture. Soil that is lacking in nutrients and air spaces (as compacted soil is) and soil that's loaded with weed seeds can wreak havoc with vegetables. It's easiest to improve soil conditions before any plants are in place, so take the time now to remove grass and weeds, have the soil tested, and add organic matter.

## Digging In

When preparing a new site for the vegetable garden, remove any sod or existing vegetation and turn over the soil to a depth of 8 to 10 inches. Yes, it's a lot of work initially, but it will be even more work if you don't do it. If you take the easy way out — that is, using a tiller to turn over the soil — be sure to rake out clumps of sod or weeds. Otherwise, weeds will become a chronic problem. Not many weeds are good eating.

### Testing, Testing . . .

At this stage in the making of a vegetable garden, there are many

*Remove sod from new garden areas
to prevent future weed problems.*

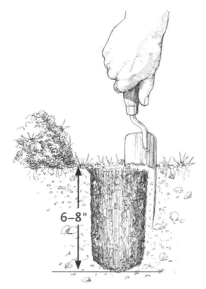

Take soil from the top 6 to 8 inches when collecting samples for testing.

Mixing soil samples from 10 spots will give a more accurate picture of the garden's pH and nutrient levels.

unknowns — for example, levels of plant nutrients in the soil and soil pH. The most important plant nutrients are nitrogen, phosphorus, and potassium. Other mineral nutrients are essential, but these three are needed in the largest amounts.

Soil pH is a measure of how acid the soil is. It's critical because it controls how much of these nutrients is available to plants. To grow vegetables, soil pH should be between 6.5 and 7.0. Well before you begin the process of preparing the garden for planting, collect a sample of soil from the garden site. To collect a sample, take a trowelful of soil from the top 6 to 8 inches of soil. Do this at 10 spots within the garden. Mix the samples in a bucket and remove a cupful of the mixed soil. Air-dry it. Place it in a clean, zip-lock plastic bag and send it to a university or private soil-testing laboratory for analysis. Typically, test results will be returned along with recommendations for how to correct soil pH and plant-nutrient levels.

### Amending the Soil

Work amendments (limestone, sulfur, fertilizer, organic matter) into the soil to a depth of 6 to 8 inches. Without a soil test, adding the right amounts of limestone or sulfur and fertilizer is just guesswork. For gardeners who prefer guessing to knowing, we recommend using natural fertilizers that slowly release plant nutrients. This reduces the chances of applying too much fertilizer, which may cause damage to plant roots.

### Organic Matters

In our opinion, the most important ingredient to add to garden soil is organic matter. Every time we started a new garden in what used to be a lawn or field, our crops grew and produced exceptionally well for the first few years. This was because high levels of organic matter had accumulated in the previously undisturbed soil from decayed grass clippings or dead plant parts. Unfortunately, as we tilled the soil, the amount of soil organic matter steadily declined each year, as did the quality of growth and yields of vegetable

Preparing garden soil for planting might seem like a lot of work, but the results are well worth the effort. If you focus at least as much attention on your garden soil as on the seeds or plants you buy, your garden will be a success.

crops. We learned the hard way about the value of maintaining a good amount of organic matter in garden soil. We now add organic matter to our garden soils every year, using a variety of methods.

### Compost

Compost is decayed organic matter. Where do you get it? You can spend a small fortune to buy compost at the garden center, or get it for free by composting yard, garden, and certain kitchen wastes (e.g., eggshells, coffee grounds, vegetable and fruit trimmings) in your own backyard.

The thought of composting is unnerving to some gardeners. They envision having to build elaborate bins or to buy expensive prefabricated composters. It becomes even scarier when they see thick volumes on the subject of composting in bookstores. Well, to paraphrase a popular bumper sticker, "compost happens." Composting does not have to be complicated. Our compost pile is just a big heap on the ground. And if it makes you feel better, we've seen in England similar compost piles hidden in remote corners of some of the most fabulous gardens in the world — no elaborate bins, no expensive rotating plastic drums, just a big mound of garden debris.

Our compost pile consists of yard, garden, and kitchen wastes. The pile is elongate, with

*Use a garden fork to work compost into soil to a depth of 6 to 8 inches.*

the most recently applied material at one end. The other end has the oldest material. We don't fuss with turning over the pile. When we need compost, we simply dig it out from the bottom of the old end of the pile. This type of compost pile is referred to as a cold pile, meaning that the composting process takes place slowly. It may take a year for the organic debris to break down, but since we're in no hurry, this suits our needs just fine.

However, some people like it hot. Those who are impatient to get a finished compost product should build or buy a compost bin of some sort. A bin confines the plant debris to a small space and the walls of the bin trap heat generated during composting. That heat speeds the composting process, as long as the pile is turned frequently (every few weeks) and is kept moist. Also, the pile should have a mix of brown organic debris such as dead plants and leaves and green materials such as fresh grass clippings. The green materials have more nitrogen than the brown material does. More nitrogen means faster composting. Frankly, that's too much for us to worry about, so we like it cold.

In late fall or early spring, we spread a 1- to 2-inch layer of compost or aged manure over the soil surface and dig it into the soil with a spading fork to a depth of 6 to 8 inches.

A *cover crop of clover between rows of corn reduces weed problems and prevents soil erosion.*

## Cover Crops

Another strategy we use is planting cover crops. We like to experiment with different cover crops and have had success with oats and winter rye in fall and buckwheat, Sudan grass, and berseem clover in summer.

If you've ever heard the term "cover crop" and thought it was something only farmers had to be concerned about, think again. Planting a cover crop is a great way to care for, improve, or renovate backyard-garden soil during the times soil is not actively involved in production of lettuce, peas, tomatoes, corn, squash, and other edibles. Cover crops are also effective during the growing season to control weeds, reduce soil compaction, and take up any plant nutrients crops don't use. Plant low-growing cover crops like clover between rows of vegetables.

**What are they?** Miscellaneous plants growing in the garden may provide cover, but a *cover crop* is a grass, legume (clover, for example), or broadleaf plant purposely grown to benefit the soil and/or other crops. A cover crop may help in one or more of the following ways:

- preventing soil loss through both wind and water erosion by keeping soil anchored in place with its roots

- capturing and using nutrients, including fertilizer left over from vegetable crops

- adding organic matter and returning nutrients to the soil when it is tilled under before planting vegetable crops

- alleviating soil compaction as its roots grow through hard, dense areas of soil

- keeping germination and growth of weeds in check by reducing the amount of sunlight reaching weed seeds and seedlings

- adding nitrogen to the soil (if you use a legume cover crop)

**Pick your cover.** The cover crop you plant depends on what benefits are important in your garden, when you plan to plant, and your ability (or desire) to work the cover crop into the soil before vegetable planting. The table on page 21 lists several commonly grown cover crops and pertinent details about planting and benefits.

In general, grasses are best for adding organic matter, since they grow faster than legumes and can produce many leafy shoots; their rapid growth also makes them good at shading out weeds. Legumes are excellent if adding nitrogen to the soil is important, since they house root-dwelling bacteria that "fix" or convert atmospheric nitrogen into a usable form for the plants; this nitrogen becomes available to crops after the legumes die and are worked into the soil. For adding both organic matter and nitrogen, use a mixture of grasses and legumes. Broadleaf plants such as buckwheat also add organic matter and can shade out weeds.

**Get growing.** Garden centers and farm stores carry cover crop seed, though possibly in quantities larger than you need at any one time. That's okay — stored cool and dry, seed can last for future plantings (though you may need to sow older seed more thickly because fewer seeds will sprout).

Once you've got your seed, prepare a planting area in the garden: Remove vegetable crop remains to the compost pile, till if necessary, and use a metal rake to level the area. Hand-scatter or use a lawn seeder to spread seed at the recommended rate (see the table on page 21, or follow the Internet link listed in Resources, page 185).

Give legume seeds a helping hand prior to planting in areas where they have not been previously planted — mix them with an inoculant of their associated nitrogen-fixing bacteria (available from seed suppliers) or buy pre-inoculated (also called rhizo-coated) seeds. Rake seeds into the soil and tamp lightly with the rake to establish contact between the seeds and soil. This contact is important for enough moisture to reach the seeds to enable germination. Keep the soil moist for a germinating cover crop, but after the crop grows a few inches tall, check the soil and watch the plants to determine whether they need to be watered. Little or no irrigation may be necessary as the plants fill in and shade the soil.

**Tilling in.** How and when to turn a cover crop into the soil varies according to the crop. Some cover crops planted in summer are killed by winter temperatures and what little is left the following spring may be turned under to a depth of 6 to 8 inches with a fork or spade or tilled into the soil. Other cover crops have extensive top growth that will need to be cut back before they can be worked into the soil. Winter rye contains compounds that may delay or prevent germination of tiny vegetable seeds if it is not incorporated into the soil well in advance of planting crops. Decaying cover crops can actually create a shortage of nitrogen in garden soil for several weeks after they are incorporated, as nitrogen is used in the decomposing process.

# Good Cover Crops for Your Vegetable Garden

| CROP | SEEDING TIME AND RATE | CUT/KILL METHOD | BENEFITS AND TIPS |
|---|---|---|---|
| **Grasses** | | | |
| **Winter rye** (*Secale cereale*) | Late summer to mid-October at 2–3 lbs/1,000 square feet | Mow in spring before seeds set (if extensive growth) and till under | • Germinates at low temperatures and can be planted later than other cover crops<br>• Cold hardy and tolerant of low-fertility soils<br>• Produces a lot of growth in spring<br>• May prevent weed-seed germination, but can also affect tiny vegetable seeds if tilled in spring too close to planting time |
| **Oats** (*Avena sativa*) | Mid-August to mid-September at 1–2 lbs/1,000 square feet | Till under in spring | • Fast-growing cover<br>• Tolerant of wet soils<br>• Winter killed |
| **Sorghum-Sudan-grass** (*Sorghum bicolor* × *S. sudanense*) | Late spring to midsummer at 1 lb/1,000 square feet | Mow during summer if needed and till under in spring or transplant vegetable seedlings into winter-killed grass | • Fast growing, but requires good fertility and moisture<br>• Excellent weed control<br>• Winter killed |
| **Legumes** | | | |
| **Hairy vetch** (*Vicia villosa*) | August to early September at 1–2 lbs/1,000 square feet | Cut in spring and till under or cut at flowering and till under | • Best nitrogen-fixing legume<br>• Produces substantial growth<br>• Mix with vetch/pea inoculant before sowing in new areas<br>• Winter hardy<br>• Can be sown with rye or oats |
| **Crimson clover** (*Trifolium incarnatum*) | Late summer to early fall at 0.5–2 lbs/1,000 square feet | Till under in spring | • Adds nitrogen to soil<br>• Not reliably winter hardy<br>• Can also be spring planted and grown as summer cover crop<br>• Use true clover inoculant before sowing in new areas |
| **Cowpea** (*Vigna sinensa*) | Early summer to late summer at 2–3 lbs/1,000 square feet | Till under at flowering or if late planting, allow to winter-kill | • Adds nitrogen to soil<br>• Develops deep taproot and is tolerant of droughty, poor soil once established<br>• Good for summer weed control<br>• Winter killed<br>• Use cowpea/peanut inoculant before sowing in new areas |
| **Other** | | | |
| **Buckwheat** (*Fagopyrum esculentum*) | Early summer to midsummer at 3 lbs/1,000 square feet | Mow and/or till under at flowering | • Fast growing, can get two crops in summer if allowed to reseed<br>• Good for summer weed control<br>• Tolerates acid soil<br>• Winter killed |

# Garden Planning
# WEEK BY WEEK

MOST PEOPLE live in regions of the country where temperatures are going to drop below freezing during the winter. Therefore, cold, frosty weather dictates much of our gardening activities: when to start plants from seed, when to prepare soils, when to plant, and when to harvest.

The dates for these activities will vary depending upon the region of the country where you are gardening. In general, the baseline date most often used to determine the timing of vegetable gardening activities is the average date of last spring frost. The week-by-week part of this book is organized in relation to that date.

**Before you go any further, find the average date of last frost for your general area. Write that date at the top of the week-by-week section titled Week of Average Date of Last Frost (page 88). Work forward and back from there, writing in the dates for each week of your gardening season.**

## Finding Your Last Frost Date

Of course, the next question is, "Where do I find the average date of last frost?" You could contact the local radio station, since many stations keep such records. However, if those folks are too preoccupied by the weekly top-20 countdown to pay attention to the weather, contact your county Cooperative Extension office, if one exists in your county — no longer a certainty due to budget cuts over the years that have downsized that agency in many states (follow the link listed in Resources, page 185, to find the office nearest you). The agricultural agent at the Cooperative Extension office should be able to tell you the average date of last frost for your area. You can also consult the table at the end of this book (see page 187); start by finding the city nearest you and then adjust the date as necessary, depending on your local geography.

## Maps and Charts

Another option to find the average date of last spring frost, as well as the average date of first fall frost, is to examine the maps and tables published by the National Climatic Data Center (see Resources, page 185). Find your location on the map or in a table and see what the average date of last frost is for that area.

However, keep in mind that "average" is not equal to "last." It means there's a 50 percent chance that the last spring frost will occur prior to that date and a 50 percent chance that frost will occur after that date. (Even with our nominal math skills, we figured that out. We also figured it out when we got too excited and put in summer crops right around the average last frost date and lost them to frosts that came after that date.) For that reason, we like the fact that the climate data provided by the NCDC also includes the average date after which there is only a 10 percent chance of frost. In practical terms for gardeners, that date is actually more meaningful than the average date of last frost. After all, do you really want to set out tomato seedlings knowing that there is a 50 percent chance they will be zapped by frost?

## Microclimates

Tables and maps are quite broad and do not recognize microclimates that influence timing of your gardening activities. Microclimates are specific areas in your yard that are affected by local conditions such as amount of light, temperature, and soil moisture. These factors are influenced by exposure to sun and wind, the slope of the land, and proximity of your garden to structures such as buildings and trees. As an example of microclimate effects, British gardens are well known for being surrounded by stone or brick walls. Why? Is it because of some obsession for privacy or aesthetics? No. The walls are warmed by sunlight and emit heat, providing protection from frost for plants in the enclosed garden.

We're not suggesting that you build stone walls around your garden, but be aware that a vegetable garden with a southern exposure may have a slightly warmer microclimate than one with a northern exposure. A garden near the foundation of a building will be more protected from cold than one in an open area. On the other hand, a garden located in a low-lying spot (e.g., a swale, hollow, bottom of a slope) may be more prone to frost than one in an upland site. These are things that you will come to know after several years of gardening experience. Therefore, you will need to make adjustments to the week-by-week schedules that we have presented in this book. It all adds to the nuances of gardening.

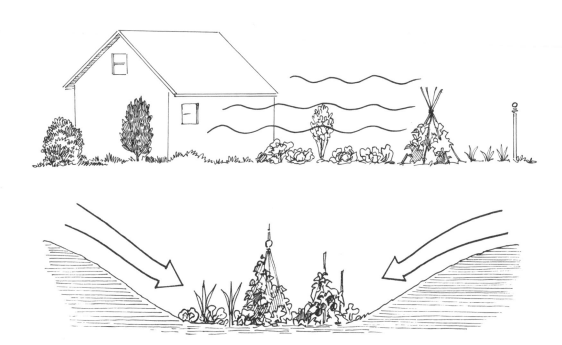

*Heat emanating from adjacent buildings and cold air flowing into low spots are examples of local conditions that can influence the average date of last frost.*

# 20–15 weeks before average date of last frost

Dates in my area:_____ to _____

## GENERAL

- Asparagus → Order crowns
- All crops
  - → Send out seed-catalog mail orders
  - → Inventory seed-starting supplies
  - → Inventory, clean, and repair gardening tools
  - → Make your own germinating mix

## MAINTENANCE

- Stored crops
  - → Remove spoiled individuals
  - → Inventory supply for what to grow more or less of this year

## SEED STARTING

- Parsley, thyme → Sow seed indoors
- Broccoli, mung bean, alfalfa → Grow sprouts indoors
- Leek, onion → Sow seed indoors for transplants
- Oregano, chive, basil → Sow seed indoors for potted plants

YEAR_____

YEAR_____

YEAR_____

# 20–19 weeks before average date of last frost

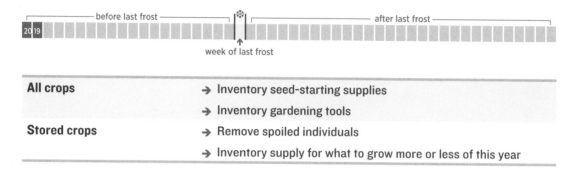

| All crops | → Inventory seed-starting supplies |
| | → Inventory gardening tools |
| **Stored crops** | → Remove spoiled individuals |
| | → Inventory supply for what to grow more or less of this year |

*I have very few gardening books, but my favorites are those that are organized either by month in the growing season or by specific crop, since I can quickly find what I need to do and when. The other "book" I rely on heavily is my own garden journal — notes from previous years are invaluable. — Jennifer*

**S**tart a garden journal. Jot down your daily observations, completed tasks, thoughts for additions or changes to the garden, and any other relevant gardening information on the journal pages provided in this book. This information will be invaluable when reviewing successes and failures you have had in the garden.

**Resolve to plant a smaller vegetable garden this year** if weeds have overtaken the garden in the past few years. Weeds rob vegetable crops of nutrients, compete for water, harbor insects and diseases, and contribute to reduced crop yields. However, we shouldn't be too critical of others' weedy gardens. There's an old Italian proverb that goes, "Criticizing another's garden doesn't keep the weeds out of your own."

**Build a collection of reference books on gardening.** Building a reference library does not have to be expensive. Excellent books can be bought at tag sales and at used bookstores. Many older books on gardening often contain more usable information than some current books, which may be nothing more than coffee-table picture books.

## Seeding and Planting

**Sort through packets of seed left over from last year.** If they've been stored properly (i.e., in a cool, dark, and dry location), most seeds will still be usable this year. Exceptions are onion, parsley, and parsnip. We usually buy fresh seeds of these vegetables each year. The expected life of other vegetable seeds is as follows: two years for beets, okra, and pepper; three years for beans, broccoli, carrots, cucumbers, lettuce, peas, spinach, and tomatoes; four years for cabbage, Swiss chard, squash, and turnips.

Because the quality of seed, manner of handling and storage, and other factors are variable, these figures are only approximations. If in doubt about the viability of any seed, place a sample of 10 seeds from each packet on dampened sheets of paper towels. Fold the sheets and put them in a plastic bag. Place the bag in a warm spot, and after 10 days, check each seed sample. If less than half the seeds are sprouted, buy fresh ones.

**Peruse seed catalogs** for inspiration on new plants and plant varieties for this year's vegetable garden. Check to see if your local garden center will be carrying the plants that catch your fancy. One of the advantages of buying plants locally is that you get to see what you're buying before laying out the cash.

**Conduct an inventory of seed-starting supplies.** Do you have enough flats or other containers for starting seeds and transplanting seedlings? Do you have a supply of sterile seed-starting mix? Do you need a heating mat to provide bottom heat for seed germination? Is lighting adequate for growing seedlings? (See Seed-Starting Supplies, page 28, for more information.)

## Harvest

**Follow the odor emanating from the basement.** It's most likely that some of the stored onions, potatoes, garlic bulbs, and winter squashes need to be culled. Cull those that are shriveled or rotted. This task should get rid of those foul odors that have continued to permeate the house for the past few weeks. (If it doesn't, consider discarding your old sneakers.) By the way, it's true that one bad apple spoils the bunch. An overripened fruit releases ethylene gas, which in turn hastens the ripening of adjacent fruit.

**Look at your remaining stores of preserved vegetables** (canned, frozen, dried, cold stored). Are you pining for more potatoes and carrots? Are you drowning in a sea of tomato juice? Adjust the amounts that you grow this next gardening year accordingly.

## TESTING SEED VIABILITY

Scatter a sample of 10 seeds on a damp paper towel.

Place the folded paper towel in a plastic bag near a sunny window or other heat source.

If less than half the seeds have sprouted after 10 days, buy fresh seed.

# SEED-STARTING SUPPLIES

IF YOU'RE FEELING BEWILDERED after a stroll through the seed-starting aisle at the garden center, this bit's for you. What do you really need to get started with seed sowing? Containers, labels and markers, seed-starting mix (*not* soil), light source, heat source, and water. You can go with the Cadillac or hatchback version of these items, and in most cases it will not make much difference to the seeds. Here are a few suggestions of what will work in each category, high-end and not-so-much.

**CONTAINERS:** plastic seed-starting kits (complete with bottom trays, divided plastic containers [known as six-packs in the nursery trade], and clear plastic humidity dome covers), open wooden or plastic trays, called flats (you can use the crates clementines are sold in), peat or coir pots, Jiffy pellets, egg cartons, yogurt cups or cottage cheese and butter tubs (cut drainage holes into the bottom of these plastic containers), newspaper pots

**LABELS AND MARKERS:** wooden or plastic labels, cut-up sections of cottage cheese and butter tub plastic lids, permanent markers, pencils, crayons

**GERMINATION MIX:** prepackaged soilless seed-starting mix, homemade mix of fine sphagnum peat moss and vermiculite (1:1 ratio)

**LIGHT SOURCE:** grow lights, cool white bulbs in fluorescent light fixtures, south- or southeast-facing sunny window

**HEAT SOURCE:** germination heat mat, heating cables or coils, soil thermometer, thermostat, warm location (such as a sunroom or a greenhouse)

**WATER:** spring water, nonchlorinated tap water, rainwater, rigid clear plastic dome or clear plastic bag to maintain high humidity before germination, watering can with small-holed sprinkling head

There are some neat gadgets out there, like precision seeding tools, which are great for sowing tiny seeds, but we're decidedly low-tech and prefer to spend our money on the seeds and plants.

*There are many choices for containers to use for seed starting, ranging from commercial products such as plastic trays, peat pots, and Jiffy pellets to recycled food containers including yogurt cups and butter tubs.*

# Heirloom Vegetables

**Ron:** One of the hottest trends in vegetable gardening in recent years is the growing of heirloom varieties. My kids think it is appropriate that an heirloom like me should be growing heirloom vegetables. The definition of an heirloom variety is a matter of debate, but most agree that an heirloom must have been around prior to 1951, when the first hybrid vegetables were introduced. So, I guess I do qualify as an heirloom.

Most people grow heirloom varieties for their flavor. Arguably, heirloom varieties of vegetables have more flavor than their modern counterparts. Yet for me, growing heirlooms is a way of connecting with the past. The heirloom varieties I grow are ones that I recall my father planting. I can still visualize him setting out transplants of 'Brandywine' and 'Marglobe' tomatoes and 'Black Beauty' eggplant and sowing seeds of 'Nantes' carrot, 'Little Marvel' peas, 'Long Green Improved' string bean, 'Golden Bantam' sweet corn, and 'Hubbard' winter squash. My mouth is watering just thinking about it.

Heirloom vegetables have become so popular that many seed companies now list varieties in their catalogs. Many garden centers sell both seeds and plants of heirlooms. So make room for a few heirloom vegetables in this year's garden.

**Jen:** *I go crazy over the descriptions of heirloom varieties in seed catalogs, so much so that when Dad and I order seed I'm tempted to ignore the excellent varieties that have been developed more recently. While 'Brandywine' remains my all-time-favorite tomato for slicing and eating raw (nothing compares on a bacon, lettuce, and tomato sandwich or in a caprese salad), its yields are inconsistent and the fruit quality is variable. Hybrids like 'Jet Star' and 'Early Girl' are really the stars in our garden. They resist disease and yield bumper crops of consistently high-quality fruit.*

# 18–17 weeks **before** average date of last frost

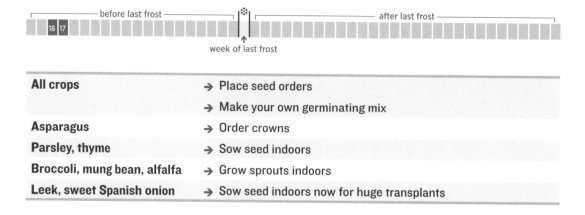

before last frost ⟶ | ❄ | ⟵ after last frost
`18` `17`

↑
week of last frost

| | |
|---|---|
| **All crops** | → Place seed orders |
| | → Make your own germinating mix |
| **Asparagus** | → Order crowns |
| **Parsley, thyme** | → Sow seed indoors |
| **Broccoli, mung bean, alfalfa** | → Grow sprouts indoors |
| **Leek, sweet Spanish onion** | → Sow seed indoors now for huge transplants |

**S**ave the mesh bags in which oranges are packaged. These mesh bags are great for storing onions, garlic, and shallots, because all of these bulbs need good air circulation for proper curing and storage. Of course, this means that you'll have to buy oranges by the bagful.

## Seeding and Planting

Plan to start some vegetables from seed, rather than buying transplants. Many gardeners have abandoned the practice of starting their own transplants. With all the nurturing that seedlings need, some folks find it easier to just buy transplants later in the season. That's okay, but the enjoyment of starting plants from seed can help you endure a long winter season.

Place seed-catalog orders early to ensure getting your choice of varieties. Pumpkin pie aficionados should look for a small pumpkin variety to make the best-tasting pie. Some choice varieties for pie making are 'Baby Bear', 'Peek-a-Boo', 'Spookie', 'Small Sugar' (our personal favorite), and 'Trickster'.

Peruse the seed racks at the garden center. Seed packets are in, and the choices are abundant. Plus, you can avoid the rising shipping and handling charges that go with catalog orders. Go with the tried and true, but also try some new varieties of vegetables and flowers. The varieties labeled as All-America Selections are always safe bets. (We view garden centers in the same way we do bookstores and hardware

stores. They are not only places to dispose of some of our financial assets, but they are also great places for browsing. We often stop by garden centers just to educate ourselves about new gardening products. Plus, our local garden center offers free seminars throughout the year, including presentations on vegetable gardening. Look for similar offerings in your own area.)

Place an order for asparagus crowns. Asparagus crown is another name for asparagus plant. Buy 1-year-old crowns of varieties that produce only male plants (asparagus plants are either male or female) and are resistant to rust and fusarium, the two major diseases of asparagus. Some choice varieties are 'Jersey Supreme', 'Jersey Knight', and 'Jersey Prince'. Planting asparagus may not be in the best interests of a beginning gardener since it takes a lot of effort to prepare an asparagus bed. However, asparagus is a perennial crop. Once planted, asparagus will produce edible spears for 20 years or more.

**Order an assortment of bean types.** Get seeds of bush beans and pole beans, and if you have room in the garden, get shell beans for drying and edible soy beans for eating fresh or for drying. With all those beans, you might also want to order a supply of Beano.

**Include chard in your seed order** if you like leafy green vegetables. Typically we make repeated sowings of seeds of leafy greens, such as spinach and lettuce, through the growing season. Also, most leafy greens are cool-season crops and tend to "bolt" (that is, send up flower stalks) in the heat of summer. On the other hand, we make only one sowing of chard; it rarely bolts and will continue to grow and produce edible leaves through the summer and well into fall.

**Order extra seed** of vegetables that you'll be sowing multiple times. It can be difficult finding seed in mid- or late summer for late-season plantings. By that time of year, garden centers generally will have sold out or taken

vegetable seeds off the shelves to make room for grass seed and spring-flowering bulbs.

**Prepare new and used seed-sowing containers in advance.** Wash containers with soap and water and follow with a rinse of 10 percent bleach (1 part bleach to 9 parts water) or hydrogen peroxide to sterilize the containers. Using disinfected containers is critical to the success of growing your own seedlings, since young plants are very susceptible to disease.

## ALL-AMERICA SELECTIONS

GENERALLY, we're advocates of the adage "If it ain't broke, don't fix it!" In gardening terms, that means we typically rely on varieties of vegetables and annuals that have performed well for us in the past. Nevertheless, we do admit to tempting fate each year by testing a few new varieties. Even then, we frequently play it safe by planting varieties selected as All-America Selections (AAS). For those of you who aren't familiar with All-America Selections, these are new varieties of seed-grown flowers and vegetables that have been chosen for their exceptional traits after being evaluated in numerous trial gardens across the country. The varieties have to do well in all sections of the country and be superior to any previous variety of its type. Very few new plants receive the All-America designation. All-America Selections are good choices for beginning gardeners because they perform well under a wide range of growing conditions.

Like other gardeners, we have to wait until the seeds of AAS varieties are marketed before we get a chance to try them. However, a few years ago, we were given seed of several AAS plants by a friend with "connections." All of the varieties performed extremely well. We especially enjoyed 'Mariachi', a medium-hot pepper shaped like a jalapeño but larger. Our plants were loaded with peppers, so many that we were able to share them with friends. One of our favorite ways to prepare 'Mariachi' peppers is to stuff them with herbed cheese or other concoctions and then grill them. As a result of our willingness to try something new, this is one variety that has now become a mainstay in our vegetable garden.

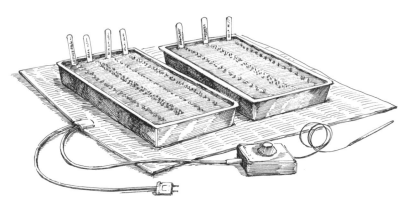

*Propagation mats are a great way to provide heat for seed germination.*

**Sow seeds of slow-growing herbs.** Parsley, thyme, and many other herbs are slow to germinate and almost as slow to grow. So, why not get an early start on these, especially if you're planning to grow them in pots? The key to growing herbs in winter is to provide plenty of light.

**Grow some sprouts in a jar for tasty salad toppers.** Easy vegetables to try are broccoli, mung beans, adzuki beans, chick peas, soy beans, and alfalfa. Be sure to use seeds that are labeled for sprouting use (don't use field seeds unless you are certain that they have *not* been treated with fungicide). You can purchase seeds for sprouts at most natural-food outlets.

**Provide a source of heat when starting seeds indoors.** Most vegetable seeds germinate best at temperatures between 70 and 80°F (21 to 27°C). Heat may come from overhead lights or a sunny window. We prefer bottom heat — that is, warmth generated by a propagation mat or heating coils placed under seed containers. With a propagation mat, the heating cables are enclosed in a rubber mat. The wires are less likely to short out and the mats are easier to handle than heating coils when setting up a propagation table.

**When starting seeds indoors, moisten the germinating mix** before filling flats and trays. Commercial germination mixes

*Seedlings that are sown thinly in flats are much easier to separate at transplant time.*

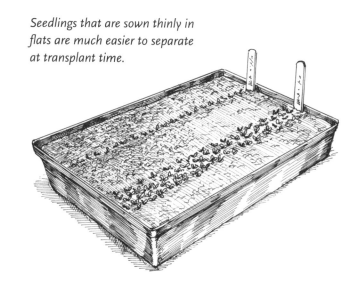

consist mostly of peat moss, which absorbs water very slowly. We save money by making our own mix: 1 part of milled sphagnum moss to 4 parts of fine vermiculite. We first put our mix in a large tub, add water, and then knead the mix a bit until it feels moist but not wet.

**Sow seeds thinly in rows if using flats to start seeds,** it will be much easier to separate the seedlings at transplant time. If the seedlings need to be thinned, you'll cause less damage to the roots of the remaining seedlings if you cut off unwanted plants at their base rather than pull them from the soil mix.

**Sow seed of leeks and sweet Spanish onion indoors.** Seed of these crops can be started later, but the early start will yield huge onions and leeks that you can brag about. Here's the plan: Sow sweet Spanish onion seed in deep (at least 6 inches) pots with a spacing of 1 inch between seeds. (Even larger onions can be grown with one seed per pot.) When onions come up, keep the soil evenly moist and feed the plants with a liquid natural fertilizer if the leaves become pale green. Bright light and cool temperatures are critical for seedling growth. Also, keep the shoots trimmed back to 4 inches to prevent the skinny leaves from flopping.

# EXTENDING THE GROWING SEASON

FOR THOSE OF US who live in cooler climes, the growing season never seems long enough. In spring, patience wears thin in anticipation of the first harvest, and in fall, the first hard freeze is met with groans of fait accompli: "If only the season had lasted a few more weeks, I could have fresh cucumbers for my cucumber–chili pepper sandwiches."

Short of moving to a warmer climate, there are a few commonsense strategies for extending the growing season.

## CHOOSE YOUR CROPS WELL

The first thing is to select crops that don't mind a little cold weather. In fact, some crops actually need cold temperatures in order to grow their best. Crops that require cold include celery, lettuce, onion, pea, radish, and spinach. Crops that don't necessarily need cold but can tolerate it are root crops (carrot, turnip, rutabaga), cole crops (broccoli, cauliflower, collard, kale, Brussels sprout), and potato.

## START EARLY

Perhaps the most obvious way to extend the front end of the season is to start plants indoors and then transplant them to the garden once the danger of frost has passed. We do this anyway with vegetables such as tomato, pepper, and eggplant, but the same can be done with many other crops (though for some vegetables, it is not practical; we would not bother with transplanting sweet corn or green beans). The biggest problem with starting plants indoors is the extra equipment required. Besides pots, you'll need sterile seed-starting mix, a source of heat such as a heating mat or heating cables, and a source of light. For light, we use several fluorescent fixtures fitted with cool-white fluorescent tubes. Don't bother with specialized grow lights; they are an unnecessary expense. Seedlings grow just as well with the low-cost cool-white tubes.

# Growing Sprouts

**Jen:** *I love growing sprouts in the kitchen, particularly in the winter, when it's a joy to see something green in contrast to all the white outdoors. Sprout growing is very easy, and something my 6-year-old can help with. Instead of using a jar, as mentioned in the tip on page 32, we put seeds in a wire colander over a shallow pie dish and enclose the whole thing in a clear plastic bag tied with a twist-tie. We moisten the seeds once or twice a day as needed, and get sprouts within a week. We use them in salads, sandwiches, and stir-fries.*

**Ron:** My wife and I have gone high-tech with our kitchen sprouts — we use a three-tiered plastic seed sprouter. That way, we can grow several types of sprouts at the same time. We run water into the top of the unit once or twice a day, and the water works its way down through each level by gravity.

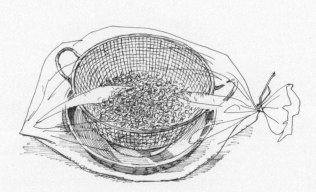

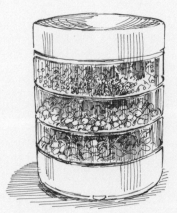

*A wire colander, pie dish, and plastic bag make a simple device for growing sprouts.*

*A triple-tiered plastic sprouter allows for growing several types of sprouts at the same time.*

# 16–15 weeks before average date of last frost

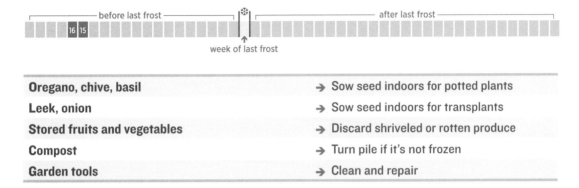

| before last frost | ❄ | after last frost |
| 16 | 15 | | |
week of last frost

| | |
|---|---|
| **Oregano, chive, basil** | → Sow seed indoors for potted plants |
| **Leek, onion** | → Sow seed indoors for transplants |
| **Stored fruits and vegetables** | → Discard shriveled or rotten produce |
| **Compost** | → Turn pile if it's not frozen |
| **Garden tools** | → Clean and repair |

Refer to notes from last spring's garden-journal entries to plan this year's vegetable garden. No journal? Okay, you'll have to rely on your memory to plan crop locations so that no crop is planted in the same spot as last year. Rotating crops each year is key to avoiding a buildup of pest populations. (See 9 Weeks Before Last Frost, page 53, for more information on crop rotation.)

## Seeding and Planting

**Sow seeds of different plants,** as well as different varieties of the same plant, in separate containers. Because of differences in germination time, seeding several varieties together makes seedling care more complicated.

**Start seeds of cold-hardy vegetables such as leeks, onions, and celery.** Seedlings of these vegetables grow slowly, so it's good to get an early start. Since they can withstand spring frosts, the seedlings can be transplanted to the garden as soon as soil is dry enough to be worked.

*Start seeds of different vegetables or varieties in separate containers to avoid problems with differences in seed-germination times.*

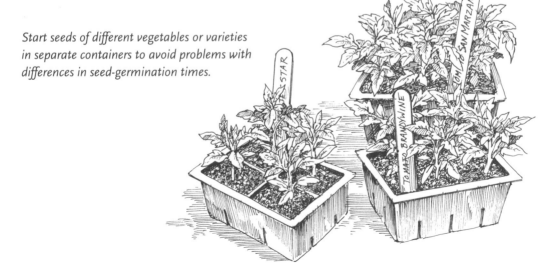

**Replenish seed-starting supplies as needed.** If you are new to seed sowing, a basic supply kit includes plastic trays (or recycled yogurt cups, cottage cheese containers, and egg cartons), wooden or plastic labels, permanent markers, and germination mix. The small wooden crates used for packaging clementines (the small, sweet-tasting oranges that are typically available through the winter) make great flats for growing seedlings.

**Include winter squash on this year's seed shopping list.** We regularly have a bumper crop of butternut squash, and our winter dinner table is frequently graced with a bowl of the creamy orange squash. Besides butternut, we plant buttercup and acorn winter squash.

**Start seeds of oregano, chives, and basil.** Though it's a little early to start most herbs that will be transplanted to the garden, it's okay to start herbs that will be grown as container plants. Some will be ready to use in culinary creations by late winter.

## Maintenance

**Turn the compost pile, if it is not frozen.** In milder climates, materials in the compost pile will continue to decompose slowly through the winter if it is turned over occasionally. By "turned," we mean using a garden fork to flip over the pile's contents.

**Clean and repair garden tools** while you have some time on your hands. Fix broken handles on shovels, hoes, and other garden tools. Then sharpen the business end of garden spades, hoes, and pruning tools.

**Find the brightest-color spray paint you can** and spray the handles of your most easily misplaced hand tools. While it's not exactly a fashionable hue, Day-Glo orange is great for locating tools in garden weeds.

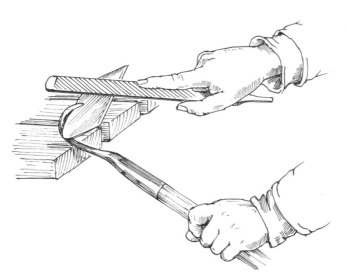

*Use a flat metal sharpening file to sharpen the outside edge of the hoe blade. Hold the file at a 45-degree angle to the hoe blade and stroke the file in one direction along the edge.*

# SOIL pH: GETTING IT RIGHT

WHILE MOST GARDENERS know that soil pH is a measure of acidity or alkalinity of the soil, they may not know why it's important to get the pH right. For one, pH determines availability of mineral nutrients to plants. Maximum availability of most mineral nutrients occurs at a soil pH between 6 and 7. That may be why most plants, including vegetables, grow best when soil pH is within that range (see the pH scale below). Another reason why soil pH is important is that beneficial bacteria and fungi — those involved in releasing nutrients from organic matter in soil, facilitating the uptake of certain mineral nutrients by plant roots, and in providing protection to plants against disease-causing microbes — occur in greatest numbers at soil pH between 6 and 7.

The first step in getting soil pH right is to have soil tested. For soil pH less than 6, it will be necessary to apply ground limestone to raise pH (reduce acidity). Laboratories that test soil pH make recommendations for the amount needed. Limestone applied to the soil surface should be worked into the top 6 inches of soil.

Lowering pH of alkaline soils — that is, increasing acidity — is a little more difficult than raising pH. Granulated elemental sulfur and sphagnum peat are the most common materials used to lower soil pH.

Because the effect of limestone, sulfur, or sphagnum peat on changing soil pH takes place slowly, it's best to have soil tested and incorporate the necessary amendment to garden soil in the fall prior to the next growing season. The effect of either limestone or sulfur on soil pH is not permanent. Therefore, it is a good idea to test soil every 3 to 5 years.

## THE pH SCALE
## AND SOME COMMONLY KNOWN SUBSTANCES

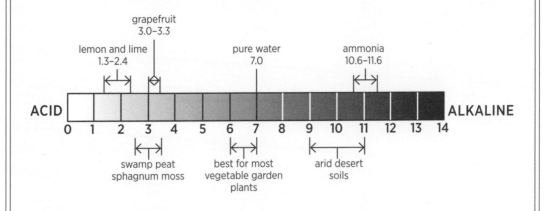

grapefruit
3.0–3.3

lemon and lime
1.3–2.4

pure water
7.0

ammonia
10.6–11.6

ACID    0  1  2  3  4  5  6  7  8  9  10  11  12  13  14    ALKALINE

swamp peat
sphagnum moss

best for most
vegetable garden
plants

arid desert
soils

# 14–10 weeks before average date of last frost

Dates in my area:_____ to _____

## GENERAL

- Cold frame → Build or buy
- Bluebird boxes → Mount near garden

## SEED STARTING

- All seedlings → Check on them daily, water as needed
- Dill, cilantro → Sow seed for indoor use
- Celery, celeriac → Sow seed indoors for transplants
- Collards, kale, lettuce → Sow seed indoors for transplants
- Cauliflower, broccoli, kohlrabi → Sow seed indoors for transplants
- Cabbage → Sow seed indoors for transplants

## MAINTENANCE

- Leftover seed → Store in a cool, dry place
- Power equipment → Tune up

## HARVEST

- Onions in storage → Use sprouting tops in cooking

YEAR_____

YEAR_____

YEAR_____

# 14–13 weeks **before** average date of last frost

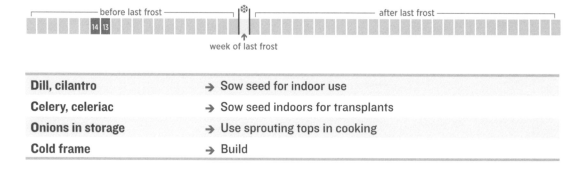

before last frost | week of last frost | after last frost

| Dill, cilantro | → Sow seed for indoor use |
| Celery, celeriac | → Sow seed indoors for transplants |
| Onions in storage | → Use sprouting tops in cooking |
| Cold frame | → Build |

Start saving recipes that call for the fruits and vegetables growing in your gardens. We have three or four favorite recipes for each crop in our gardens. This saves us the trouble of having to think much about how to prepare vegetables that we are harvesting at a given time. (The cookbooks Jennifer turns to most often are like the gardening books she finds useful — they are conveniently organized by vegetable. See Resources, page 185.)

**Buy a soil thermometer.** This step requires a modest investment, but it yields invaluable help in determining when to plant crops outdoors. The time to plant many crops is dependent upon not only air temperature but soil temperature as well. For example, cucumbers should not be planted until after danger of frost has passed *and* when soil temperature reaches at least 60°F.

**Build a cold frame to extend the growing season at both ends.** Cold frames containing soil are great for planting salad greens in fall; empty cold frames are useful for hardening off seedlings before moving them to the garden in spring. (See Hardening Off, page 62, for more information about cold frames.)

*A simple cold frame can be made of lumber with a slanted glass cover.*

### Seeding and Planting

Sow seeds of dill and cilantro in large pots for indoor growing. These two, like most herbs, thrive in bright light, so put the pots in the sunniest window of your home.

Start celery and celeriac indoors. Celery and celeriac are slow growers and won't be ready for transplanting to the garden for 10 to 12 weeks.

### Maintenance

Replace the bulbs in plant lights if they are several years old. Properly operating fluorescent lights hung 4 inches above seedlings and left on for 14 hours a day give great results. Seedlings will be dark green, short, and sturdy — ideal for transplanting.

### Harvest

Don't throw away onions that are sprouting in storage. Use the sprouting shoots as you would scallions or green onions. However, it is a good idea to separate the sprouting onions from the nonsprouting ones. We sometimes pot up a few of the sprouting ones. They'll continue sending up green shoots for several weeks before surrendering.

*Save sprouting onions and use the shoots in cooking.*

## STARTING SEEDS IN A CONTAINER

1. Fill a flat or other container with moist, sterile germination mix (to within an inch of the rim); shake and gently tamp to level the mix.
2. Sow seeds in rows or scatter seeds on soil surface.
3. Cover seeds with moist germination mix, to a depth equal to three times their size, and gently tamp to ensure good seed-to-soil contact.
4. Label the flat and water with a fine-rose watering can or spray bottle. Cover the flat with plastic (or place entire flat inside a clear plastic bag), and place it in a warm location (best temperatures for germination are 70 to 80°F [21 to 27°C]). After the seedlings germinate, place the flat under cool white fluorescent lights.

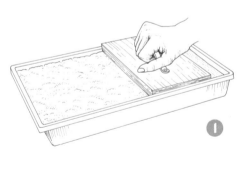

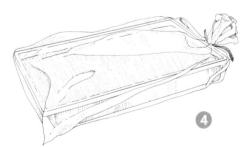

# In Praise of Celeriac

**Ron:** Though I have in hand the seed packets for vegetable crops I want to grow this year, my plan keeps changing. Every time I peruse a seed catalog, I'm captivated by the eloquent description of some vegetable not on my original plan. For example, celeriac is described in one catalog as "most common in France in the Céleri-rave remoulade, a tasty appetizer . . ." I don't have a clue what that dish is, but it sounds good enough to make me add celeriac to my seed order.

It's been several years since I've grown celeriac, but I recall it being much easier to grow than celery. Celeriac, also known as knob celery or celery root, is a strain of celery native to Europe. It is grown for its swollen, gnarly root, however, rather than for its leaf stalks. The bulbous part of the root grows at soil level and has a rough brown skin but white interior. As one might expect, celeriac tastes like celery, but without the stringiness. The skin has to be peeled before the vegetable can be used. Because celeriac has a growing season of 120 days, it is best started from seed indoors. Transplant seedlings to the garden when they are 2 to 3 inches tall (10 weeks after sowing). They are quite hardy and will withstand spring frosts if properly acclimated before transplanting. The only trick to growing celeriac is to give it plenty of water through the summer.

*Jen: Okay, this is a new one for me, but since I'm a fan of celery in the kitchen, I'll go along with it. Often, Dad and I will have a heart-to-heart about what we plan to grow in a given year. This is when our garden journals come in handy — if our notes indicate that something was a hassle to grow the previous year or that we didn't really enjoy eating it, we cross it off the list. With a new (or new to us) vegetable, I like to make sure it's something that we'll have plenty of use for in the kitchen, or that we can pass on to friends and neighbors when we tire of eating it day in and day out.*

Celeriac has the flavor of celery but is grown for its swollen root rather than for leaf stalks.

# NO-TILL GARDENING

A FAVORITE QUOTE of ours is one by Miles Morland in his book *A Walk Across France:* "When you stop learning, the arteries start to harden fast." Now, that alone should stimulate blood flow. However, with further concern for promoting cardiovascular health, we offer a minicourse, Soil Management 101, for your learning pleasure.

The first lesson is drawn from an experience in our vegetable garden but was inspired by the no-till practices that have long been advanced by the Natural Resources Conservation Service (formerly Soil Conservation Service) of the U.S. Department of Agriculture. Basically, "no-till" means leaving the soil undisturbed after harvesting a crop.

After harvesting our tomato crop one year, we pulled up the plants but did not turn over the soil as we usually do. We weren't thinking no-till at the time; we were just too lazy to turn it over. We also left in place the thick layer of straw that we had used to mulch the plants.

The following spring, when it came time to plant summer and winter squash, we decided to transplant the seedlings that were grown in peat pots into the area where the tomatoes had previously grown — we typically rotate our tomato crop on a 4-year cycle with garlic and shallots, squash, and corn. Noticing that the straw was still intact, we chose to leave it in place and plant the seedlings through the straw, à la the no-till system.

The result was very gratifying. Besides saving ourselves some serious exertion, we had an outstanding crop of squash, a minimum of weeds, and a noticeable increase in the number of earthworms inhabiting the soil.

This should not be surprising since no-till conserves the qualities of soil favorable to good plant growth. No-till prevents soil erosion, decreases soil compaction, prevents the pulverization of soil particles, and slows depletion of organic matter.

Practicing no-till gardening is something we should do more often, particularly since our garden is situated in a very windy location and any uncovered soil is subject to wind erosion. Another way to practice no-till in the garden is to plant transplants through winter-killed cover crops. (See Cover Crops, page 19.)

# 12–11 weeks before average date of last frost *14–21*

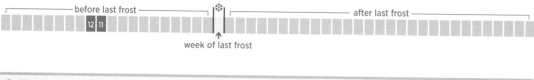

before last frost | ❄ | after last frost

week of last frost

| Collards, kale, lettuce | → Sow seed indoors |
| Seedlings | → Check on them daily, water as needed |
| Bluebird boxes | → Mount near garden |

Keep an eye out for sales on large garbage cans. Garbage cans will make inexpensive rain barrels to capture water at downspouts. Droughts are not uncommon these days, and good gardeners should always practice water conservation.

**Mount bluebird nesting boxes near the garden.** Bluebirds (and other birds, for that matter) are useful at keeping insect pests like grasshoppers and caterpillars at bay.

**Save your seed catalogs.** In addition to pictures, catalogs contain excellent cultural information on plants.

**Head to the library or Internet** to read about methods of managing pests in the landscape and garden that are safe to the environment and to your health. (See Resources, page 185, for some of

*Bluebird houses mounted on posts near the garden invite bluebirds, which feed on many garden pests.*

our favorite pest reference books and Web sites.) Safe pest management has become a lot easier these days with the development of "bio-rational" pesticides. These pesticides are typically derived from nature and usually affect only the target pest.

## Seeding and Planting

**Fill a garbage can with water and keep it in the basement** or wherever vegetable seedlings are being grown. This way, there will always be a supply of room-temperature water that can be applied to tender seedlings. Cold water slows growth and development of seedlings, and slow growth makes them more susceptible to damping-off disease.

**Keep an eye, maybe two, on seed trays.** As soon as seeds can be seen sprouting, move the trays to a spot with bright light. If you are using fluorescent lights, set them up no more than 3 or 4 inches above the tops of seedlings. Cool white fluorescent tubes are best for lighting seedlings because they give off less heat than warm white tubes.

**Keep a third eye out for damping-off disease on seedlings.** Damping-off is a destructive disease that attacks seedlings. (See Damping-Off, page 46, for more information.)

## DARK SOIL = WARM SOIL

DARK-COLORED SOILS absorb more heat than do light-colored soils, and fertile soils high in organic matter stay warm longer than do impoverished soils. Cold soils slow down root (and subsequently shoot) development. Gardeners with dark, fertile soils can get started earlier in the season — another good reason to add compost and manure to your garden soil every year!

**Sow seeds of lettuce indoors.** Follow seed-packet directions. Lettuce germinates fine with a light soil covering. Seedlings will be ready to transplant to the garden in 4 or 5 weeks, depending on the condition of the soil. (The soil should be dry enough to be worked; see Is Your Soil Workable? page 63.) You should be able to harvest some leaf lettuce about 6 or 7 weeks after they have been transplanted.

**Start seeds of collard and kale indoors.** Otherwise, wait until the soil is workable and then direct-seed lettuce, kale, and collards into the vegetable garden.

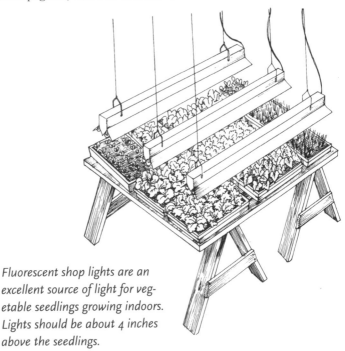

*Fluorescent shop lights are an excellent source of light for vegetable seedlings growing indoors. Lights should be about 4 inches above the seedlings.*

# DAMPING-OFF

**D**AMPING-OFF sounds like an alternative bathing practice for someone with an aversion to showers or baths. Unfortunately, it is a bit more of a serious issue for gardeners who start their vegetable plants from seed indoors. Damping-off is a general term for diseases that attack seedlings in the early stages of their development. Visual symptoms of damping-off include the sudden collapse of a seedling, and constriction and discoloration of the stem at the soil line. Several fungi cause damping-off, but for practical purposes you don't need to know which fungus is causing damping-off, since the methods of prevention are the same:

**1.** Thoroughly wash with soap and water any containers to be used for seed starting. Then wipe the surfaces with a paper towel dampened with hydrogen peroxide or a 10 percent bleach solution.

**2.** Use a sterile seed-starting mix. We germinate seeds in a mix of fine-grade vermiculite and milled sphagnum moss. After seeding, we cover the surface of the mix with a thin layer of milled sphagnum moss.

**3.** Don't crowd seeds when sowing. Thin seedlings if they are crowded.

**4.** Avoid overwatering. Use only containers with drainage holes, and don't leave the containers standing in water for any length of time. Allow the surface of the seed-starting mix to dry a little between applications of water. Remove plastic covers from seed trays after germination to lower humidity levels around the seedlings. (Diseases thrive in a humid environment.)

**5.** When transplanting seedlings, handle each one by its leaves and not the stem, to avoid damaging the stem. Injured stems are more susceptible to damping-off.

**6.** Grow seedlings in a well-ventilated area and in bright light.

**7.** Immediately discard any containers with infected seedlings. Damping-off diseases can spread rapidly to infect other seedlings.

*Damping-off is the most common disease of seedlings started indoors. Symptoms include sudden collapse of the seedling and constriction and discoloration of the stem at the soil line.*

# 10 weeks before average date of last frost

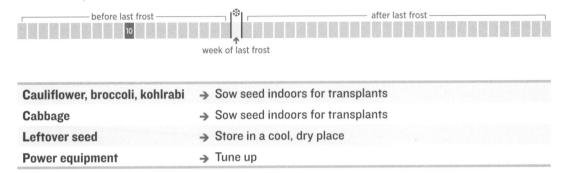

before last frost ———————— | after last frost ————————
10
↑
week of last frost

| | |
|---|---|
| **Cauliflower, broccoli, kohlrabi** | → Sow seed indoors for transplants |
| **Cabbage** | → Sow seed indoors for transplants |
| **Leftover seed** | → Store in a cool, dry place |
| **Power equipment** | → Tune up |

**B**uy a carpenter's apron. It comes in handy for holding seed packets, labels, pencils, and other accessories as you prepare seed trays. A carpenter's apron is cheap, and some lumberyards may even give one away free when you buy lumber. This may be a good time to build a treehouse or, better yet, a cold frame to harden off seedlings. (See Hardening Off, page 62.)

## Seeding and Planting

**Start seed of cauliflower, broccoli, and kohlrabi.** These plants grow fast. Except for people who live in igloos, most folks live in houses that are too warm to keep these seedlings from getting leggy. Place them under bright light in a cool location (like the basement). If you've built a cold frame, move the plants in when they are about 4 inches tall.

**Place seedlings in a cold frame** and they'll become healthy, stocky

plants. The cold frame also helps in acclimating them for the eventual move to the garden.

**Start seeds of cabbage.** Try different types of cabbage, such as green to use for coleslaw, red for salads, Savoy for stuffed cabbage, and late cabbage for sauerkraut: an entire year's menu of cabbage!

Store leftover seed properly and it should stay viable until next year. No matter how large a garden we plant, we always have unused seed. After all, who needs 55 zucchini plants when five will feed half the town? Unused seed will stay viable longer when stored in a dry, cool environment. Here's the method we use.

First unfold and lay out a stack of several facial tissues. From a freshly opened box,

*Weak, leggy seedlings (left) result when plants are grown in poor light at very warm temperatures. Seedlings growing in bright light at low temperatures will be stocky and healthy-looking (right).*

remove 2 tablespoons of powdered milk and deposit it on one corner of the tissue stack. Fold and roll the tissues to make a small pouch. Secure the pouch with tape or a rubber band and put it in a wide-mouth canning jar. Drop in leftover seed packets, seal the jar, and place it in the refrigerator. The powdered milk packet will absorb any excess moisture in the jar. After 6 months, replace the old packet of powdered milk in the canning jar with a fresh one. With this technique, seeds of some vegetables may be saved for several years.

## Maintenance

**Tune up cultivators, tillers, and other power equipment.** Change the oil, replace spark plugs, tighten bolts, sharpen the mower blade, replace hopelessly dirty air filters, and clean debris from engine parts. Fall is a better time for equipment maintenance, but late winter and early spring give procrastinators a second chance. If equipment still won't start, kick the tires to relieve your frustration, and then haul it off to the shop for repairs. Don't wait too long, because everyone else is doing the same thing!

*Save leftover seed packets by placing them in a canning jar along with a prepared packet of powdered milk. The powdered milk absorbs moisture that would shorten the storage life of seeds.*

## FROM ASH TO DUST

FOR YEARS we've dusted certain vegetables in the garden with wood ash for the purpose of repelling flea beetles, which feed on our crops. We thought that was a pretty clever and original way of organically controlling pests. Only recently have we learned that such dusts were among the earliest pesticides used by humans. So much for originality.

However, what *is* original in the realm of dusts used for pest control is kaolin, a naturally occurring clay. Scientists at the U.S. Department of Agriculture have found that an engineered form of this clay can be sprayed onto fruit and vegetable crops to suppress many insects and a few diseases. Once kaolin dries, it forms a fine film of white dust on leaf surfaces. This film acts as a barrier to both insects and certain foliar diseases. The dust can be easily wiped off fruit and vegetables when harvested. Even if some residue remains on the food, it should be of no concern since kaolin is nontoxic. In fact, kaolin is used as an anticaking agent in processed foods and is a common ingredient in toothpaste and many medicines. Read the label for lists of crops on which it can be used, and the pests and diseases that it controls. We can tell you that flea beetle is on the list.

# THEME GARDENS

IF YOU'RE A MORE EXPERIENCED gardener, you may want to design your vegetable garden differently this year. Allow space for some plots planted around a theme — in each plot, plant vegetables common to a particular ethnic cuisine. In the Italian plot, include plum tomatoes, basil, fava beans, Romano beans, broccoli raab (rapini), radicchio, arugula, and Florence fennel. For Oriental dishes, plan a plot with soybeans, Chinese cabbage, snow peas, pak choi, bunching onions, and daikon radishes. For those with a taste for Latin American cuisine, set aside a plot for tomatoes, black beans (turtle beans), an assortment of chili peppers, sweet peppers, and cilantro. In our Polish plot, we'll plant horseradish, cabbage, horseradish, potatoes, horseradish, onions — oh, did we mention horseradish? — and kielbasa. Okay, so kielbasa doesn't grow on plants. Clearly, Mother Nature missed an opportunity there.

*If you favor a particular ethnic cuisine, plant part of the garden to vegetables commonly used in that culture. Here is an Italian-theme garden with relevant vegetables.*

# 9–7 weeks before average date of last frost

Dates in my area: *March 7* to *March 21*

## SEED STARTING

| | |
|---|---|
| ▪ Pea, spinach | → Sow seed outdoors if soil is workable |
| ▪ Carrot, beet, leaf lettuce, spinach, green onion | → Sow seed in the ground if soil is workable; if not workable, sow in a container |
| ▪ Eggplant | → Sow seed indoors for transplants |
| ▪ Pepper, sweet and hot varieties | → Sow seed indoors for transplants |
| ▪ Anise, parsley, summer savory, fennel, chervil | → Sow seed indoors in individual peat pots for easier transplanting |
| ▪ Parsnip | → Sow seed in garden as soon as soil is workable |

## PLANTING

| | |
|---|---|
| ▪ Asparagus | → Plant crowns in garden |
| ▪ Horseradish | → Plant roots or crowns in garden |
| ▪ All vegetable seedlings started indoors | → Transplant to larger containers when first set of true leaves appears |

## MAINTENANCE

| | |
|---|---|
| ▪ Soil | → Prepare for planting by incorporating organic matter, wood ash, fertilizer |
| | → Spade in or till under cover crops before planting vegetable crops in garden |
| ▪ Asparagus | → Fertilize existing plants |
| ▪ Garlic, strawberry beds | → Remove half of mulch covering if plants are showing signs of growth |
| ▪ Raised beds | → Build and grow vegetables in them where soils are poor |
| ▪ Onion | → Shear seedling tops if they're getting floppy |
| ▪ Lettuce, onion, leek | → Put indoor seedlings in cold frames to harden before planting in garden |

## HARVEST

| | |
|---|---|
| ▪ Horseradish | → Dig roots, harvest young leaves |

YEAR_____

YEAR_____

YEAR_____

# 9 weeks before average date of last frost

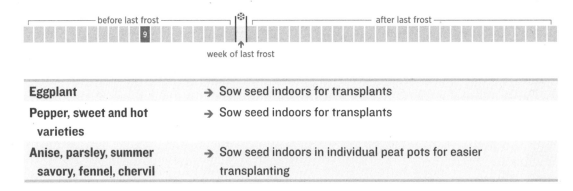

before last frost | ❄ | after last frost

9

↑
week of last frost

| Eggplant | → Sow seed indoors for transplants |
|---|---|
| Pepper, sweet and hot varieties | → Sow seed indoors for transplants |
| Anise, parsley, summer savory, fennel, chervil | → Sow seed indoors in individual peat pots for easier transplanting |

*Turn a large garbage can into a homemade rain barrel. Note the hole in the lid, the screen over the hole to exclude leaf debris, and the spigot attached at the base of the barrel.*

**P**lan to use crop rotation in the garden to reduce disease and insect pest occurrence. For example, avoid planting cabbage and related crops in the same area of the garden each year. This will help prevent clubroot, a serious disease of these crops. (See Crop Rotation, page 53.)

## Seeding and Planting

**Start seeds of eggplant and hot and sweet varieties of pepper.** Although related to tomatoes, these vegetable crops are started a week or two before our tomatoes, since peppers and eggplant are slow growers. Also, we won't set out the transplants until nighttime temperatures remain above 55°F because they're more sensitive to cold nighttime temperatures than tomatoes are.

Sow seeds of anise, parsley, summer savory, fennel, and chervil in individual peat pots because they do not transplant well from flats. Add some coarse sand to seed-starting mixes that are high in peat moss. The roots of these and other herbs do not like prolonged exposure to wet soil.

## Maintenance

**Prepare for a dry growing season.** Though it's difficult to predict rainfall patterns for the entire season, it's always good to plan for drought by enriching garden soil with water-holding organic matter, selecting drought-tolerant vegetables for sites with very sandy soil (see Drought-Tolerant Vegetables, page 54), and capturing rainwater by placing rain barrels beneath downspouts. Even if rainfall is normal, employing these practices will not hurt a thing.

March 11, '15
fertilizer on garden, aspargus, herbs
woodash on garden

2015

Trays

*handwritten annotations:* purple spinach · lettuce (black simpson) · onion · Cilantro · Daikon Radish · Broc. rapini · circular hole

# CROP ROTATION

ONE OF THE SIMPLEST WAYS to reduce incidence of disease and certain insect pests in the vegetable garden is crop rotation. The goal of rotation is to avoid planting the same or related vegetables in the same area of the garden in successive years.

Among the common vegetable families are the crucifers (cabbage, broccoli, cauliflower, turnip, radish, kohlrabi, mustard); the cucurbits (melon, cucumber, squash); the

solanaceous plants (tomato, pepper, potato, eggplant); and the legumes (bean, pea). Root crops, such as carrot, beet, and onion, can be lumped together for the purpose of crop rotation. The idea is to not plant a member of a given family in the same spot where another member of that family grew in the previous year. When it comes to growing vegetables, don't stagnate — rotate!

*handwritten annotations:* arugula · cabbage · caro? · turnip · beets · circular & rectangular hole.

## Typical Crop Rotation

| PLOT A | PLOT B | PLOT C | PLOT D |
|---|---|---|---|
| **YEAR 1** | | | |
| Tomatoes, potatoes | Carrots, beets, parsnips, spinach, lettuces | Cabbage, Brussels sprouts, cauliflower, rutabaga | Onions, garlic, leeks, peas, beans |
| **YEAR 2** | | | |
| Onions, garlic, leeks, peas, beans | Tomatoes, potatoes | Carrots, beets, parsnips, spinach, lettuces | Cabbage, Brussels sprouts, cauliflower, rutabaga |
| **YEAR 3** | | | |
| Cabbage, Brussels sprouts, cauliflower, rutabaga | Onions, garlic, leeks, peas, beans | Tomatoes, potatoes | Carrots, beets, parsnips, spinach, lettuces |
| **YEAR 4** | | | |
| Carrots, beets, parsnips, spinach, lettuces | Cabbage, Brussels sprouts, cauliflower, rutabaga | Onions, garlic, leeks, peas, beans | Tomatoes, potatoes |

# DROUGHT-TOLERANT VEGETABLES

"DROUGHT TOLERANT" may not be the best term to describe vegetables that can get by during extended dry periods. For continuous growth and good yields, all vegetables need some water, especially early in their growth cycle, for good seed germination and root development. However, once established, there are vegetables and varieties that can be productive with less water than is required by other crops. Typically these are warm-season crops and those that develop deep root systems. Most drought-tolerant vegetables originated in areas where dry summers are common, such as Mexico, the Mediterranean region, and the southwestern United States.

*Straw mulch around this pepper plant conserves soil moisture and helps the plant to continue good growth during periods of drought.*

Here is a list of vegetables that can remain productive during dry periods:

Asparagus
Asparagus bean
Cowpeas (black-eyed peas)
Eggplant
Melons
New Zealand spinach
Okra
Peppers
Rhubarb
Squash
Sweet potatoes
Tepary beans
Tomatoes
Woody-stemmed herbs (oregano, rosemary, sage, thyme, winter savory)

When shopping for these vegetables, keep in mind that some varieties are more drought tolerant than others, so read the variety description carefully.

Despite the ability of these vegetables to tolerate dry conditions, good gardening practices that help retain soil moisture should not be overlooked. Annual incorporation of organic matter, mulching, and weed control are essential elements in getting the best production from vegetables, even during the driest of times.

# 8 weeks before average date of last frost

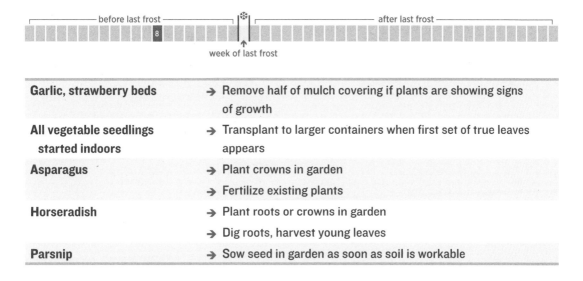

before last frost — 8 — week of last frost — after last frost

| Garlic, strawberry beds | → Remove half of mulch covering if plants are showing signs of growth |
| --- | --- |
| All vegetable seedlings started indoors | → Transplant to larger containers when first set of true leaves appears |
| Asparagus | → Plant crowns in garden |
| | → Fertilize existing plants |
| Horseradish | → Plant roots or crowns in garden |
| | → Dig roots, harvest young leaves |
| Parsnip | → Sow seed in garden as soon as soil is workable |

## Seeding and Planting

**Transplant vegetable seedlings to larger containers** when they have developed their first set of true leaves. This set of leaves appears to be the second set of leaves since the first set is actually the seed leaves, or cotyledons. The seed leaves are typically fleshy and show little resemblance to the true leaves. When transplanting, hold a seedling by its leaves, not its stem. Fungi that cause damping-off disease are too easily spread by touching seedling stems.

**Plant horseradish.** While we don't want to discourage anyone from growing horseradish, it is a vegetable best suited to cool regions of the country. Also, it is not a vegetable for folks with a tender palate.

**Plant asparagus.** It's a long-lived perennial crop. Some asparagus beds have been known to remain productive for 50 years or more. When shopping for asparagus roots, select a variety such as 'Jersey Giant', 'Jersey Knight', or

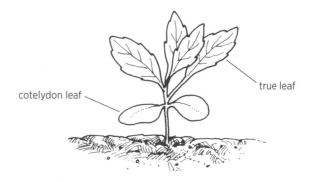

cotelydon leaf

true leaf

*Seedlings are ready for transplanting from seed flat to larger container when the first set of true leaves appears. Handle seedlings by their true leaves when transplanting.*

*Check under winter mulch for signs of growth of garlic. Immediately remove half the mulch layer if garlic shoots are emerging. Remove the remaining mulch in about 7 days if weather permits.*

'Jersey Prince', because these are resistant to rust and fusarium, two diseases that can devastate an asparagus crop. (See Planting Asparagus from Crowns, page 59.)

**Sow seeds of parsnips** as soon as garden soil is dry enough to be tilled. Parsnips have a long growing season. We don't expect to harvest them until late fall.

**Turn your garden spade or hoe into a measuring stick** for determining planting distances and

*Make measurement markings on the handle of a hoe; 2-inch intervals for the first foot and then 6-inch intervals thereafter.*

row width. Using paint or an indelible pen, mark distances on the handle of the hoe or spade. No sense in carrying more tools than are needed.

## Maintenance

**Take a peek under winter mulches,** whether it is mulched strawberry beds or rows of fall-planted garlic. If plants are showing signs of growth (our garlic is often actively growing at this time of year), remove about half of the mulch covering and leave it between the rows. Wait 7 to 10 days and then remove the rest, but only if the weather is relatively mild. We like to keep the mulch handy in case hard freezes, below 28°F (–2°C), are forecast. In that situation, we put the mulch back in place for as long as temperatures are below freezing.

**Fertilize the asparagus bed** with a natural fertilizer such as fish meal, or apply compost or aged manure. If using fertilizer, follow label directions for amounts to apply. With manure or compost, spread about a 1-inch layer over the ground. Use a garden fork to work these amendments well into the soil.

## Harvest

**Dig up horseradish roots** for grating (see In Praise of Horseradish, page 57). Young leaves of horseradish make a tasty addition to salads.

# In Praise of Horseradish

**Ron:** Horseradish is one of the traditional foods served in Polish homes at Easter. Horseradish roots can be bought at most grocery stores, but it has been a long-held ritual in our family to dig up fresh roots in early spring. When I was barely knee-high to a grasshopper, I would accompany my father on his annual trek to dig up roots in the wild. The "wild" in this case were the drainage ditches bordering our onion fields. We would bring home an armful of the roots and then grate them by hand, a task that was done outdoors, preferably with gale-force winds at our backs. The grated horseradish was then packed in jars with a brine made by boiling equal parts vinegar and water plus some salt. The horseradish to be served with ham and kielbasa at Easter was colored purple by the addition of beet juice. Though my father is gone and the family no longer farms, I carry on the tradition by digging horseradish roots growing in my garden.

*Jen: The passion for horseradish has skipped a generation in our family. I am ambivalent about the stuff, but my son can't seem to get enough of Grandpa's homemade horseradish. I do know that horseradish plants are mighty tough to kill. When we moved into our home, Dad gave us some horseradish roots for the garden. I planted a few (mainly to keep the Polish family tradition going) but forgot the rest, which remained next to the compost pile in a plastic bucket. The soil-covered roots sprouted new shoots. The bucket filled with water, and the plants continued to flourish. The roots I did plant in the garden are in a neglected area choked with weeds, yet they have all survived.*

# PLANTING HORSERADISH

PLANT HORSERADISH from roots or crowns. A horseradish crown is the top portion of a root where the leafy shoot emerges. You can buy crowns or roots at retail garden centers or by mail order, but don't overlook the possibility that a friend may be growing horseradish and is willing to give you some pencil-sized roots or some crowns for planting in your garden. You won't need more than a few roots or crowns. Horseradish grows fast. Therefore, we suggest planting your horseradish in an isolated corner of the garden near other perennial vegetables such as asparagus and rhubarb. Horseradish has a tendency to spread and can quickly become a weed problem when it mingles with annual vegetable crops.

Horseradish is not fussy about soil as long as it is planted in *deep* soil. We've grown horseradish in heavy soils, sandy soils, and everything in between, so we never bother with any special soil preparation. When planting horseradish as roots, we dig holes to a depth equal to the length of each root plus 2 inches, then drop a root into a hole and cover with soil. When planting horseradish crowns, we place each crown in the soil so that the top is just below ground level.

*Plant horseradish roots in a hole as deep as the length of the root plus 2 inches. If the root is attached to the crown, be sure the crown is just below ground level and the leaves above ground level.*

# PLANTING ASPARAGUS FROM CROWNS

ASPARAGUS can be started from seed, but it is much easier to start with 1-year-old plants, called crowns. When buying asparagus crowns, select male hybrids since modern hybrids are disease resistant and male asparagus plants tend to produce larger spears than do female plants.

Besides being a very tasty vegetable, the great thing about growing asparagus is that you should have to plant it only once. The normal expectation is that an asparagus bed will remain productive for 20 to 30 years, but we've heard of beds that have been going strong for more than 50 years.

There are many versions of the proper planting method for asparagus. Here's how we did ours. First, we had the soil tested for pH. Asparagus does not like acid soils, so we had to add limestone to bring our soil pH to 7. Next, we dug a trench that was about 12 inches wide and 8 inches deep, using our eyeball measurement technique. (If your soil is sandy, make the trench a little deeper. If the soil is heavy, make it shallower.) In the bottom of the trench, we added a 2-inch layer of compost and a smattering of rock phosphate and wood ash. Aged manure can be used in place of compost, if you can find an aged cow or horse. If you have a penchant for precision, get a complete soil test and follow the recommendations for fertilizer application. Our combination of compost and handfuls of rock phosphate and wood ash worked well, and we didn't obsess about precision.

Once our trench was prepared, we placed the asparagus crowns in the bottom of the trench, spreading the roots of each plant as we went, though there's no need to get fussy about this; the roots will grow down and the shoots will grow up no matter how you place them. We spaced the crowns 18 inches apart. For our family of five, we planted 25 crowns in two rows separated by 5 feet, as measured from center to center. After the crowns were set, we covered them with several inches of soil. As the plants grew, we continued to add soil to cover the shoots until the trench was completely backfilled. It is our understanding that current research has shown that the trench can be filled in right after planting and gradual backfilling is not necessary as long as the soil is not compacted.

Once established, asparagus is one of the more drought-resistant vegetables, but during the first year, we recommend watering the bed deeply once each week if Mother Nature is not providing adequate amounts of rainfall.

*Asparagus is a perennial crop grown from crowns (plants) set out in trenches and then covered with soil.*

# 7 weeks before average date of last frost

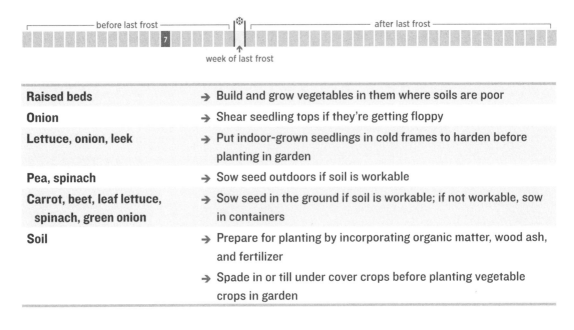

before last frost — | ❄ | — after last frost

7

↑
week of last frost

| Raised beds | → Build and grow vegetables in them where soils are poor |
| Onion | → Shear seedling tops if they're getting floppy |
| Lettuce, onion, leek | → Put indoor-grown seedlings in cold frames to harden before planting in garden |
| Pea, spinach | → Sow seed outdoors if soil is workable |
| Carrot, beet, leaf lettuce, spinach, green onion | → Sow seed in the ground if soil is workable; if not workable, sow in containers |
| Soil | → Prepare for planting by incorporating organic matter, wood ash, and fertilizer |
| | → Spade in or till under cover crops before planting vegetable crops in garden |

**B**uild raised beds where soils are not particularly well suited for growing vegetables. The sides of raised beds can be constructed from cement blocks, bricks, decay-resistant wood such as cedar or locust, or one of the new composite products made from wood wastes and recycled plastic. Fill the beds with topsoil enriched with compost.

## Seeding and Planting

**Plant peas and spinach if soil is workable.** Areas with heavy clay soils may not yet be workable (see Is Your Soil Workable? page 63). Covering seeded rows with floating row covers will hasten seed germination and protect seedlings from harsh winds (see Floating Row Covers, page 69). Anyone who had the forethought to make raised beds last year probably has a good chance of being able to sow seed of these and other cold-hardy crops now. The rest of us will have to peer over the fence and wish we had been so clever.

*Carrots, lettuce, and other cold-hardy vegetables can be grown in patio pots if garden soil is not workable in early spring.*

Start some vegetable crops in containers, especially if soils are too wet to work. Carrots, beets, leaf lettuce, spinach, and green onions are cold-hardy vegetables that can be planted in containers now. Use commercial potting soil or make a potting mix of screened compost and coarse sand. Never use garden soil alone in containers, since it will quickly become compacted.

## Maintenance

Spread wood ash over the garden before incorporating organic matter in preparation for spring planting. Apply ash at a rate of 2½ pounds per 100 square feet. (2½ pounds equals ½ gallon). Do not apply wood ash to soils with a pH of 7 or greater.

Incorporate organic matter (aged manure or compost) into garden soils in preparation for planting. If soils are poorly drained and still wet, however, wait awhile longer before doing this. Soils that are rich in organic matter are a hedge against drought because of the ability of organic matter to absorb and hold on to water. Improve the drainage of heavy garden soils by working in limestone, sand, and large quantities of organic matter. Plan to make additions of organic matter to these soils an annual event.

Apply a natural fertilizer when preparing garden soil for planting vegetable crops. The actual

---

### CHEATING MOTHER NATURE

THOUGH COOL-SEASON CROPS can tolerate cool air temperatures, their early development may be slowed by cold, wet soils. Planting in raised beds can overcome these deterrents to growth. Soils in raised beds drain quickly and temperatures may be as much as five degrees warmer than that of the surrounding soil. Raised beds can be made simply by mounding soil in narrow berms that are about 6 inches higher than the surrounding soil. Ideally, this should be done in late fall so that the beds are ready for early spring planting.

---

nutrient content of natural fertilizers varies depending on the sources used in the product. Therefore, it's not possible to make a general recommendation about how much fertilizer to add; you'll need to read the label before applying.

Avoid applying high-nitrogen fertilizers or fresh manure to areas of the garden where beets, carrots, radishes, and turnips are to be grown. Too much nitrogen will promote leaf growth at the

expense of root development. Fresh manures will also promote scab on beets.

Continue to shear the tops of onion seedlings growing in flats if they are getting long and starting to flop. Cut back seedlings to 4 inches and use the trimmings in salad dressing and stir-fry dishes, or to flavor soups and stews. That's one of the things we love about onions: you can use them at any stage of their growth cycle.

*Shear to 4 inches the tops of onion seedlings growing in flats.*

**Get cold frames ready to receive seedlings** that were started indoors. Cold frames are used to harden off or gradually acclimate seedlings to outdoor conditions.

*Gallon-size milk jugs inside a cold frame will absorb heat and protect tender seedlings on frosty nights.*

Put cold-hardy seedlings such as lettuce, onions, and leeks in the cold frame first, for about 2 weeks before transplanting in the garden. When nighttime temperatures are averaging above freezing, put tomatoes and other warm-season crops into the cold frame. Be prepared to throw some burlap bags or blankets over the glass top if frosty weather threatens. We like to keep several gallon-size, clear plastic bottles filled with water in the cold frames. On sunny days, the water absorbs heat and provides warmth for tender seedlings on frosty nights. A little blue or green food coloring in the water enhances its ability to collect solar heat.

## HARDENING OFF

SINCE THE INDOOR ENVIRONMENT is so different from the outdoors, plants started indoors will need to undergo some acclimation before they are planted out in the garden. This can be done by moving plants outdoors to a partially shaded location for a few hours the first day and then gradually increasing the time and exposure by a few hours each day. After 7 to 10 days, the plants can be moved to their permanent location in the garden.

The easiest method of acclimating seedlings for the move to the garden is to place the plants in a cold frame 7 to 10 days prior to planting in the garden. There are many variations on the structure of cold frames.

Commercial cold frames can be purchased through catalogs or at local garden centers and come in a variety of sizes, structural materials, and price tags. Some of these even have devices that automatically open the lid of the cold frame when temperatures get too high on sunny days. (As people who have cooked a few crops by failing to open cold frames on warm, sunny days, we appreciate this feature. Yet we can't see spending money on something that can be built so easily without much expense. Our cold frame is reconstructed every year from cement blocks and old storm windows. It works very well, but we do have to monitor temperatures regularly.)

# Is Your Soil Workable?

**Ron:** When is it appropriate to begin working the soil? Many areas of the country may still be enjoying mud season. This is due either to heavy, poorly draining soils or to the fact that some frost is still in the ground. Whatever the reason, soils that are wet should be left alone. Tilling or walking on wet soil destroys its structure and increases its density. Plant roots have a difficult time penetrating such soil.

To determine if soil is workable, pick up a handful of soil from the garden and squeeze it in your hand. If water drips from the soil or if the soil remains in a firm clump after you release your hand, the ground is still too wet to be worked. If the clump of soil breaks apart with gentle prodding, it is okay to grab a spading fork and begin turning over the soil in preparation for planting. (That's a little trick I first learned by watching Hoot Gibson and the sodbusters in old western movies.)

*Jen: I have no idea who Hoot Gibson was, but I guess he was on to something with the handful-of-soil trick. It's better than my way — if I take one step into the garden and end up with a few inches of soil stuck to the bottom of my shoe, it's too wet!*

*To test soil for workability, squeeze a handful. Upon releasing your hand, soil that is too wet will remain as a solid clump; soil that is too dry will immediately fall apart; soil that is just right will crumble with gentle prodding of your thumb.*

# 6–4 weeks before average date of last frost

### Dates in my area:_____ to _____

## SEED STARTING

| | |
|---|---|
| • Lettuce, chard, kale, endive, carrot, radish, beet, kohlrabi, turnip, parsnip | → Sow seed outdoors in prepared garden soil |
| • Mustard greens | → Sow seed outdoors in garden |
| • Tomato | → Sow seed indoors |
| • Basil | → Sow seed indoors to grow transplants |

## PLANTING

| | |
|---|---|
| • Onion | → Plant sets, hardened-off transplants, or seeds outdoors if soil is workable |
| • Leek | → Put hardened-off transplants in garden |
| • Potato | → Plant (if you've got the space) |
| • Herbs | → Plant several types in a large strawberry jar |

## MAINTENANCE

| | |
|---|---|
| • All crops | → Start weeding |
| • All vegetable seedlings indoors | → Water carefully and provide adequate light |
| • Rhubarb | → Divide crowded crowns and replant |
| • Rosemary | → Make new plants by layering |
| • Cabbage, broccoli, cauliflower, Brussels sprouts | → Harden-off transplants in a cold frame or sheltered outdoor location before planting in garden |

YEAR_____

YEAR_____

YEAR_____

# 6 weeks before average date of last frost

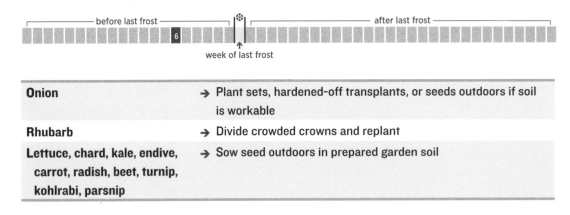

before last frost — ❄ — after last frost

6

week of last frost

| Onion | → Plant sets, hardened-off transplants, or seeds outdoors if soil is workable |
|---|---|
| Rhubarb | → Divide crowded crowns and replant |
| Lettuce, chard, kale, endive, carrot, radish, beet, turnip, kohlrabi, parsnip | → Sow seed outdoors in prepared garden soil |

Set up a rain gauge near the garden to monitor rainfall through the growing season. As a rule of thumb (or any other finger, for that matter) vegetable gardens should get the equivalent of 1 inch of rainfall per week. Apply water only if Mother Nature falls short of that goal.

## Seeding and Planting

**Plant onions from sets, hardened-off transplants, or seed.** Sets are small, dry onions. We have found that onions we plan to store after harvest are best started from seed or plants. As you gain more experience, you'll find that onions started from sets don't store well.

**Sow seed of leafy greens** (lettuce, chard, kale, endive) and root crops (carrot, radish, beet, kohlrabi, turnip, parsnip). Mix some sand with tiny vegetable seed to make sowing easier. Another technique is to mix fine seed in very soft gelatin. Put the gelatin/seed mix in a squeeze bottle and squeeze out the mix down the middle of a prepared row.

**Plant radishes within the row** or between rows of carrots or beets. This technique, called interplanting, allows for optimal use of garden space. The radishes will

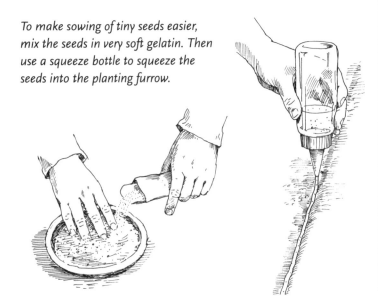

*To make sowing of tiny seeds easier, mix the seeds in very soft gelatin. Then use a squeeze bottle to squeeze the seeds into the planting furrow.*

be harvested before the carrots or beets begin competing with them for space, water, and nutrients. Typically, fast-growing vegetables are interplanted with slow-growing types. Leaf lettuce interplanted with tomatoes and squash paired with pumpkins are two examples of warm-season candidates for interplanting, but that planting is still weeks away. (See Space-Saving Gardening, page 12, for more on interplanting and wide-row planting.)

# HOT CAPS AND CLOCHES

A FEW DEVICES that allow for early transplanting are hot caps and cloches. These have been around since Adam and Eve planted their first tomato in the Garden of Eden near the apple tree where the snake lived. A hot cap is a small, dome-shaped structure of wax paper that is placed over each transplanted seedling. It acts as a mini-greenhouse, protecting a transplant from light frosts while also warming the soil. Cloches are similar but typically are made of more expensive materials, such as glass and translucent plastic. Unlike hot caps, which last only one season, cloches are reusable. Also look for some newer devices such as the Wall-o-Water, which are plastic cylinders that can be filled with water. Frugal gardeners can come up with alternatives to hot caps and cloches using household items such as large transparent plastic milk or soda bottles.

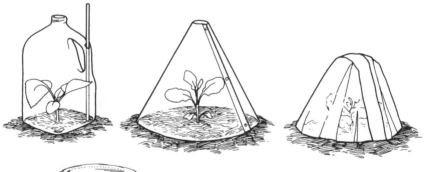

*An assortment of hot caps and cloches can be used to protect vegetable transplants.*

**Save space by planting leafy crops, root crops, and onions in wide rows.** Sow seeds of these vegetables in 18- to 24-inch-wide bands rather than single rows.

## Maintenance

**Divide crowns of rhubarb plants that have become crowded.** When a rhubarb plant begins to get large with crowded leaf stalks (around 5 years old), or whenever you want additional plants, you can divide it. Dividing is best done in early spring, preferably while the plant is dormant. You will divide the crown, the portion of the rhubarb plant with buds and roots attached.

# RHUBARB POWER

ACCORDING TO A STUDY done by the U.S. Department of Agriculture, rhubarb outperforms cranberries in several nutritional categories. Rhubarb contains more potassium, calcium, folic acid, beta-carotene, magnesium, and vitamins A and K than cranberries. (That's good news, because we weren't looking forward to flooding our backyard every time the cranberries were ready for harvest. Rhubarb is so much easier to grow.)

**1.** Dig up the entire crown with a garden fork or spade. Try to get as much of the root system as possible.

**2.** Using your hands, a spade, or a small ax, divide the crown into sections, each piece containing at least one bud and a portion of roots.

**3.** Mix a shovelful or two of compost into the soil where you plan to plant the divisions. Make a hole slightly larger than a crown piece and put the piece in the hole with buds facing up. Fill in the hole with soil, burying the crown 1 to 2 inches below the surface.

**4.** Mark the location where each crown is planted until new shoots appear above the soil surface.

**5.** Just as with new rhubarb plants, remember to let the divisions grow for a year before you begin harvesting leaf stalks again.

*Use a spade or an ax to divide the crown of a rhubarb plant.*

# FLOATING ROW COVERS

THE WEATHER IN THE SPRING is . . . well, springlike. It rains, a few snow-flakes fly, and then the sun shines; it is hot one day and then cool or cold for the next 5 or 6 days; and the wind at times is fierce and relentless.

What's a gardener to do?

Use floating row covers. They are the great moderator of variable weather conditions. Floating row covers are made of spun plastic, such as polypropylene, and feel similar to and have a texture like tissue paper. They are called "floating" row covers because of their lightness. Placed over vegetable crops, row covers seem to float above the plants.

Though made of plastic, floating row covers enable sunlight, water, and air to pass through. Row covers transmit about 85 percent of sunlight — enough to support plant growth and to warm cool spring soils. They can protect tender transplants from light frosts, down to about 28°F (–2°C). They also help soil retain moisture and protect trans-plants from the ravages of spring winds.

Studies have shown that most vegetable crops produce earlier and larger yields when plants are covered with row covers early in the season. We have had a great deal of success in our own garden using row covers to protect transplants. We have to remember to remove the covers from cool-season crops once daytime temperatures are consistently above 80°F (27°C), though. Row covers should also be removed from insect-pollinated crops, such as cucumbers, squash, and melons, when the plants are in bloom. Row covers, if handled carefully, can provide several years of use.

If you are met with blank stares when you ask for floating row covers at a garden center, try asking about all-purpose garden fabric.

*Floating row covers protect crops from the vagaries of fickle spring weather and can result in earlier and larger yields of many crops.*

# 5 weeks before average date of last frost

before last frost ── ❄ ── after last frost

5

↑
week of last frost

| All crops | → Start weeding |
|-----------|-----------------|
| **Leek** | → Put hardened-off transplants in garden |
| **Potato** | → Plant (if you've got the space) |
| **Tomato** | → Sow seed indoors |
| **Basil** | → Sow seed indoors to grow transplants |
| **Rosemary** | → Make new plants by layering |

## Seeding and Planting

**Transplant leek seedlings** into a 4-inch-deep trench, spacing the seedlings 4 to 6 inches apart. As a beginning gardener, you may ask why we give spacing recommendations in ranges, such as 4 to 6 inches apart. It's because we don't always walk around the garden carrying a ruler or our hoe with the marked handle (see page 56). Spacing requirements aren't all that precise, so often we eyeball our spacing, but keep it within a reasonable range for each particular crop. As you gain experience, spacing becomes second nature.

**Start seeds of tomatoes indoors.** Studies have shown that tomato seedlings that are 6 to 8 weeks old when transplanted provide the best growth and highest yields of fruit. Grow a mix of varieties: an early-yielding variety; a large beefsteak type for sandwich making or for juice;

*Plant leek seedlings into a 4-inch-deep trench.*

an heirloom variety for great taste; an Italian plum tomato for roasting, drying, and sauce; and a cherry or grape type for snacking and for salads. Midsize tomatoes are best for tossing at political rallies.

**Plant potatoes, if there's room in the garden.** Potatoes are not a crop for small gardens. Plant potatoes from so-called seed potatoes, which are actually pieces of whole potatoes. Each piece contains at least one "eye," or bud.

Stems grow from eyes. Plant potato pieces about 4 inches deep and 10 inches apart in rows 2 feet apart. Early-season varieties such as 'Norland', 'Anoka', and 'Irish Cobbler' are great to plant now, but wait until last frost

## PLANTING POTATOES

1. Cut seed potato into sections, with each section containing at least one eye.

2. Dig a 5-inch-deep furrow and place a 1-inch-deep layer of compost in the bottom.

3. Set potato sections into the furrow, with 10-inch spacing between sections. Cover with soil.

date to plant late-season varieties, such as 'Superior', 'Katahdin', and 'Kennebec'. Late-season varieties are best for winter storage. For something different and very tasty, try the yellow potato 'Yukon Gold'. There is also a variety of blue potato, 'All Blue'.

**Start seeds of basil indoors for garden transplants.** Large-leaf sweet basil varieties such as 'Genovese' and 'Italian Large Leaf' are most popular with home gardeners, but for some variation in color and flavor, consider other types of basil, including purple basil, lemon basil, Thai basil, and spicy basil.

**Propagate potted rosemary plants** by layering the stems. Simple layering is done by bending a stem to the potting soil surface (or ground, if you're lucky enough to be able to grow rosemary outdoors) and then covering part of it with soil. After several weeks, roots will form on that portion of the stem. Sometimes, plants will do the work for you, since their branches normally develop roots where they touch the soil. Cut off the rooted section of stem from the parent plant, dig it up, and repot.

## Maintenance

**Avoid using manure as a soil amendment** where potatoes are to be planted, because it increases the chances of scab disease on the tubers. Scab is also more likely to occur in soils with a high pH.

**Begin weeding.** Perennial weeds such as quackgrass and winter annual weeds such as common chickweed and pennycress grow vigorously in the cool weather of spring. Winter annuals are weeds that come up in late summer or early fall and then flower the following spring or summer, after which they die. It is important to get these weeds out of the garden now, before they flower and set seed.

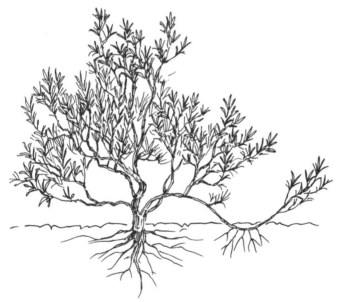

*Create a new rosemary plant by layering a stem.*

# STICKY TRAPS FOR INSECT CONTROL

WE'LL ADMIT IT. We've got sticky fingers. (Hmmm, that sound we just heard must be the neighbors locking up their treasured possessions.) Anyway, our sticky fingers are the result of handling yellow sticky traps. Since we don't like using pesticides in the vegetable garden, we often resort to alternative methods of controlling pests on vegetable crops. The yellow sticky trap is one option that works well on certain insect pests.

A yellow sticky trap is nothing more than a bright yellow plastic board that is coated with a nondrying sticky material. Commercially made sticky traps are available at most retail garden centers. However, it's relatively easy to make your own traps from thin plywood, plexiglass, or metal cut to a size of about 8 by 12 inches and painted with a bright yellow paint. Coat these with a sticky substance, such as Tack Trap or Tanglefoot. Mount sticky traps in various locations in the garden.

Aphids, whiteflies, and many other insects locate plants to feed on by using visual cues such as color reflected from plant leaves. While we may see leaves as green, these insects can distinguish between individual colors of light, such as varying hues of yellow and blue, reflected from plant leaves. A major component of the light reflected from plant surfaces is in the yellow range of the spectrum, and young leaves reflect more yellow than older leaves do. Interestingly, most of the aforementioned insects prefer younger or newer growth to feed on and are drawn to this growth by the reflected yellow color. Sticky traps work by attracting the insects that are drawn to the yellow color. When the insects land on the trap, they get stuck in the sticky coating.

Though recommended as a monitoring device for detecting the presence of specific insects, a yellow sticky trap can be used as a control device when pest populations are small. In the vegetable garden, sticky traps can be used to control whiteflies, leafhoppers, flea beetles, leaf miners, and (some say) aphids (we haven't had much luck using the traps against them).

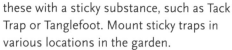

*We like to attach sticky traps to bamboo stakes with a clothespin that has been securely taped to the stake.*

# 4 weeks before average date of last frost

before last frost ────────────────── | ❄ | ────────────── after last frost ──────────────

| 4 |

↑
week of last frost

| Herbs | → Plant several types in a large strawberry jar |
| Cabbage, broccoli, cauli-flower, Brussels sprout | → Harden-off transplants in a cold frame or sheltered outdoor location before planting in garden |
| Mustard greens | → Sow seed outdoors in garden |
| All vegetable seedlings indoors | → Water carefully and provide adequate light |

## Seeding and Planting

**Use a large strawberry jar for planting a minigarden of herbs.** A strawberry jar is a clay pot with several planting pockets in its sides. Be sure to include

*A large strawberry jar will make a mini-garden of culinary herbs.*

oregano among the herbs planted. Researchers with the U.S. Department of Agriculture found that herbs are higher in cancer-fighting antioxidants than fruits and vegetables are, and oregano had the most antioxidants. That's good news for us pizza lovers.

**Harden off cabbage, broccoli, cauliflower, and Brussels sprout transplants** for 7 to 10 days before planting them in the garden. Harden off plants you started from seed indoors as well as transplants bought at garden centers. If you don't have a cold frame, place transplants outdoors in a sheltered spot (away from direct sun and wind) for about 2 hours the first day. Gradually increase the amount of time and exposure to sun each day thereafter.

**Sow seeds of mustard greens in the garden.** The peppery flavor of mustard leaves will put a little zip in your salads. Mustard is usually planted as a spring and fall crop since the plants tend to bolt (send up flower stalks) in hot weather. A close relative of mustard greens, called mustard spinach, has better tolerance to heat. Plant both types of greens for a longer harvest.

**Water seedlings of tomatoes** and other vegetables started indoors, but be careful not to overwater. Over-watering is one of the primary causes of seedling failure. Feel the soil surface of seedling containers. If it feels moist, do not water.

**Keep transplants compact** and sturdy by giving them adequate light. If this is a problem, place a reflective screen (such as aluminum foil) behind tomato, pepper, and other seedlings growing in pots on windowsills. The reflective foil helps redistribute light over plant leaves and prevents plants from becoming too leggy.

*A foil-wrapped piece of cardboard placed behind seedlings growing on a windowsill will reflect light onto the seedlings for better growth.*

## GROWING STURDIER SEEDLINGS

Jennifer's son, Liam, has this habit of gently "petting" the tomato seedlings that are growing in flats in the sunroom. He seems to enjoy the tactile sensation, and apparently so do the seedlings. According to research done at the New York State Agricultural Experiment Station, tomato seedlings that bend or flex periodically will grow into sturdier plants than those couch-potato seedlings that don't get a workout. It sounds a bit like witchcraft, but this actually works.

It is not uncommon for seedlings grown indoors to become weak and spindly. However, a light brushing of seedlings several times each day results in transplants that are stocky and sturdy. This brushing can be done carefully by hand (smokers should wash their hands thoroughly to avoid spreading tobacco mosaic virus to seedlings). For anyone without a curious youngster in the house, try using a dowel or pencil to gently brush the tops of tomato seedlings a couple of times a day for about a minute. This technique also works with other vegetable seedlings, but don't try it with brittle plants (such as peppers) or ones that are a bit sticky, like lettuce. Another option is to set up a small fan to simulate a light breeze blowing over the seedlings. The key is to get seedlings to bend as they would if exposed to wind. Keep in mind that using a fan will dry the seedling growth medium, so be prepared to water more often.

*Brushing tomato seedlings regularly with a dowel or other implement will result in sturdier plants for transplanting.*

# 3–1 week before average date of last frost

Dates in my area:_____ to _____

## SEED STARTING

- Cold-hardy crops: pea, cauliflower, onion, lettuce, spinach, chard, kale, root crops → Sow seed in the garden if you haven't gotten around to it yet
- Cabbage, broccoli → Make a second sowing indoors for transplants to set out later in the season
- Squash, melon, cucumber, gourd → Sow seed indoors in individual peat pots
- Cilantro, dill → Make another sowing indoors in pots
- Leafy greens (arugula, leaf lettuce, mâche) → Sow seed in wide blocks in the garden
- Bush bean → Tempt fate — make a first sowing in garden

## PLANTING

- Strawberry → Start a garden bed with bare-root plants

## MAINTENANCE

- All crops → Watch for cutworms
- Indoor vegetable seedlings → Apply fertilizer to soilless mixes
- Beet, carrot, parsnip, onion → Thin seedlings directly seeded in garden
- Spinach, beet, chard → Protect plants from leaf miners
- Cabbage, broccoli, cauliflower, radish → Control flea beetles on plants
- Leafy greens, chard, spinach → Thin garden seedlings
- Tomato → Begin hardening off transplants in a cold frame or other protected outdoor area
- Garlic → Water regularly
- Potato → Hill soil against plants

## HARVEST

- Rhubarb → Begin harvesting stems
- Asparagus → Begin harvesting spears, but not from first-year plants

YEAR_____

YEAR_____

YEAR_____

# 3 weeks before average date of last frost

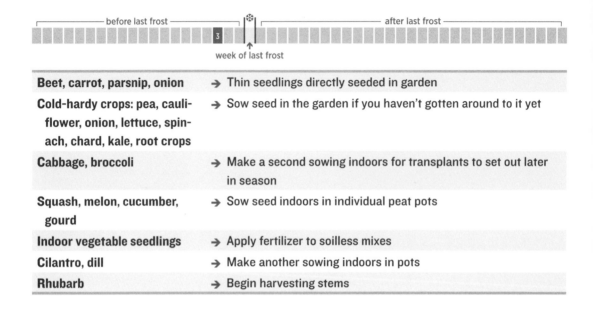

| | |
|---|---|
| **Beet, carrot, parsnip, onion** | → Thin seedlings directly seeded in garden |
| **Cold-hardy crops: pea, cauliflower, onion, lettuce, spinach, chard, kale, root crops** | → Sow seed in the garden if you haven't gotten around to it yet |
| **Cabbage, broccoli** | → Make a second sowing indoors for transplants to set out later in season |
| **Squash, melon, cucumber, gourd** | → Sow seed indoors in individual peat pots |
| **Indoor vegetable seedlings** | → Apply fertilizer to soilless mixes |
| **Cilantro, dill** | → Make another sowing indoors in pots |
| **Rhubarb** | → Begin harvesting stems |

*Pre-sprouting seeds indoors before sowing early-season crops in the garden can be a time-saver.*

## Seeding and Planting

**Sow seed of cold-hardy vegetable crops** including peas, cauliflower, onions, lettuce, spinach, chard, and root vegetables such as carrots, beets, and radishes. To make up for the lost time spent standing around admiring spring bloomers, try presprouting seeds of these vegetables.

**Start another batch of cabbage and broccoli indoors.** Plant six plants of these vegetables every 3 or 4 weeks to keep a steady supply coming along throughout the growing season. That's much better than having the entire crop mature at the same time. (We like cabbage, but having it twice a day, every day, for 14 days is more than our digestive tracts can tolerate.)

**Start seedlings of squash, melons, and cucumbers** indoors under lights or in a cold frame. The seeds of these crops germinate quickly and the seedlings grow fast. They'll be ready to transplant to the garden 1 to 2 weeks after the frost-free date. Sow seeds in peat pots, two seeds per pot to ensure that at least one good seedling emerges. If good fortune is with you and both seeds germinate, snip off the smaller of the two seedlings.

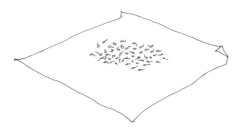

**1.** Soak the seeds in water for a few hours.

**2.** Roll up in damp paper towels. Put the paper towels into plastic zip-lock bags. Seal and label each bag.

**3.** The seeds should sprout within a few days, and they are ready for planting as soon as growth is visible. *Caution:* Seeds are very vulnerable at this point — keep them moist and handle them carefully to avoid damaging the emerging seedlings.

**4.** Mix 2 tablespoons of cornstarch with 1 pint of water and boil until it thickens into a gel. Cool and pour the gel into a plastic bag. Carefully add the germinated seeds. Turn the bag upside down a few times to distribute the seeds throughout the gel.

**5.** Cut a small hole in a corner of the bag to dispense the seeds. Gently squeeze out the seeds one at a time into a prepared garden furrow, as you would if seeding normally. The gel protects the sprouted seeds from drying out.

*Use a sharp knife or scissors to snip off extraneous seedlings in a peat pot.*

When the seedlings are ready to be set out in the garden, plant the pots and all. Because roots will grow through the walls of peat pots, it's not necessary to remove the plants from their pots. As such, expect little or no transplant shock. Peat pots, molded from a mixture of sphagnum moss and wood fiber, are biodegradable (but aren't we all).

**Start seedlings of gourds indoors.** Originally grown by ancient civilizations as a utilitarian crop (the fruit was used for containers, utensils, musical instruments, and food), gourds are used mostly as ornamentals today. They grow as spreading, rambling vines, and we recommend that they be grown on a trellis, particularly in small gardens. Gourd fruits come in an array of colors and bizarre shapes. They are great fun for young gardeners.

**Apply fertilizer to seedlings started indoors,** especially if they were started in a mix that did not contain any plant nutrients. The easiest fertilizer to use to give seedlings a boost is a liquid feed. Look for a natural product such as fish emulsion or seaweed extract.

**Make another sowing of cilantro and dill in pots.** We start new pots of cilantro and dill every few weeks because the plants tend to bolt (send up flowering stalks) rather quickly. Once they bolt, the foliage becomes sparse, and it is the foliage we want now in our cooking.

*Thin root crops so that you can fit three fingers between adjacent seedlings.*

## Maintenance

**Thin root crops,** including beets, carrots, parsnips, and direct-seeded onions, by cutting unwanted seedlings at soil level. As a rule, we thin these crops so that we can fit three fingers between adjacent seedlings.

## Harvest

**Begin harvesting rhubarb.** Along with asparagus, horseradish, and Egyptian onions, rhubarb is one of the first crops harvested in spring. These four crops are good companions since they are all long-lived perennials. (However, we don't recommend combining them in a casserole.) To harvest rhubarb, grab a stem near the base and gently pull it off. Use only the stalk, not the leaf itself.

# IN PRAISE OF RHUBARB

Let's talk about rhubarb. It is a vegetable, at least in technical terms. Nevertheless, we use rhubarb in dessert dishes. It certainly goes well in combination with strawberries, raspberries, apples, and other fruit.

Don't have any rhubarb? Plant some. Dig a large hole, set in a rhubarb plant so that the crown is about 2 inches belowground, and then backfill with soil that has been amended with ample amounts of well-rotted manure. Space plants about 3 feet apart.

Newly planted rhubarb should not be harvested this year and for only 1 or 2 weeks next year, and then up to 10 weeks after that. When harvesting, try not to remove more than a third of the stems on one plant.

To harvest rhubarb, pull off the leaf stems rather than cutting them. Less damage is done to the plants when the leaf stems are pulled off. Cutting creates a large wound that can allow for entry of disease-causing fungi.

We'll continue harvesting rhubarb until the end of June or until we get tired of rhubarb crisp, rhubarb crumble, rhubarb crunch, rhubarb cake, strawberry-rhubarb pie, rhubarb jam, rhubarb sauce, rhubarb custard . . .

Oh, as an afterthought, if a flower stem should emerge from a rhubarb plant, cut down the stem. It contributes nothing to the plant except that it means the plant may need to be divided (early next spring) or is in need of some soil enrichment, preferably with rotted manure or compost.

*Harvest rhubarb by pulling leaf stems from the plant; do not cut the stems.*

*Remove any flower stems that appear on rhubarb plants.*

# 2 weeks before average date of last frost

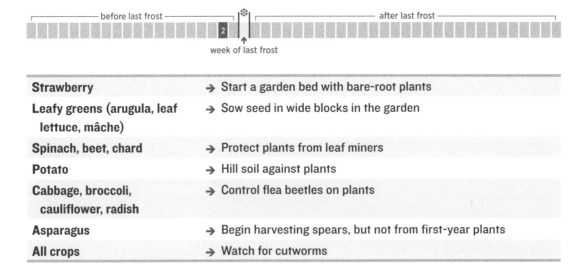

before last frost — ❄ — after last frost

**2**

↑ week of last frost

| | |
|---|---|
| **Strawberry** | → Start a garden bed with bare-root plants |
| **Leafy greens (arugula, leaf lettuce, mâche)** | → Sow seed in wide blocks in the garden |
| **Spinach, beet, chard** | → Protect plants from leaf miners |
| **Potato** | → Hill soil against plants |
| **Cabbage, broccoli, cauliflower, radish** | → Control flea beetles on plants |
| **Asparagus** | → Begin harvesting spears, but not from first-year plants |
| **All crops** | → Watch for cutworms |

Set up a mailbox in the garden. Don't expect a postal delivery, but a mailbox in the garden is a great place to keep at the ready hand tools, twine, labels, markers, plastic bags for harvesting, and other frequently used garden supplies.

## Seeding and Planting

**Plant strawberries.** Strawberries are sold as bare-root plants. Plant in soil enriched with plenty of rotted manure or compost. Make planting holes wide enough that roots may be spread out. Set plants just deep enough that the crowns are at ground level. Space plants 2 feet apart in rows that are 4 feet apart. That means you'll need 50 plants per 100 feet of row. Fifty plants should yield between 50 and 75 quarts of fruit. Yum!

## PROPER PLANTING DEPTH FOR STRAWBERRY PLANTS

**TOO DEEP**

**JUST RIGHT**

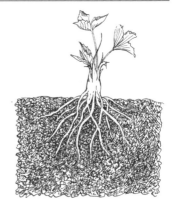

**TOO SHALLOW**

Seed an assortment of leafy greens like arugula, leaf lettuces, and mâche in wide rows. An easy way to accomplish such a diverse planting without having to buy a dozen different seed packets of greens is to look for packets labeled MESCLUN.

## Maintenance

Protect spinach, beet greens, and chard from leaf miners by keeping plants covered with a row cover, cheese cloth, or other fine screening. The adult fly stage of the leaf miner lays her eggs in midspring on the undersides of leaves. The maggots, which hatch from these eggs, feed on tissue between upper and lower leaf surfaces, leaving behind telltale trails, or "mines," in the leaves. Pick off and discard any mined leaves.

*Blotchy trails are created by leaf miners feeding on spinach leaf.*

## SCALLION SUBSTITUTES

THE SCALLIONS YOU BUY at the supermarket are typically a non-bulb-forming type of onion called evergreen bunching onion. Seeds of bunching onions can be bought at retail garden centers for spring sowing. However, don't expect to be harvesting any scallions real soon; they take a while to develop.

Fortunately, we have better alternatives for our scallions. In fact, we've already been harvesting them for several weeks at this point. Ours come from a perennial onion called Egyptian onion or top onion. The latter name refers to the bulblets that develop at the top of tall stems later in summer. Right now, we're cutting off some shoots of Egyptian onion that started coming up almost a month ago. When the necks of these shoots get a little too large for using in recipes that call for chopped scallions, we'll switch to cutting shoots from shallots we planted earlier this spring. For impatient people like us, Egyptian onions and shallots are better sources of scallions than are bunching onions.

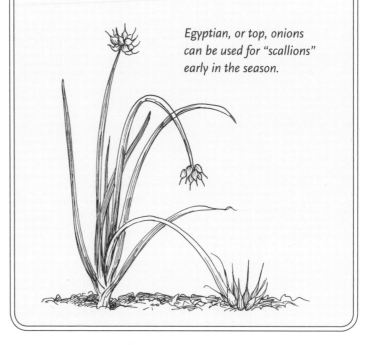

*Egyptian, or top, onions can be used for "scallions" early in the season.*

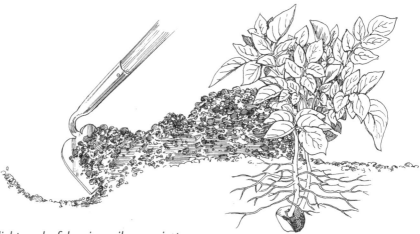

*A garden hoe makes light work of drawing soil up against young potato plants, a process called hilling.*

*Flea beetles chew tiny holes in cabbage leaves.*

**Begin hilling potato plants** when they are about 5 inches tall. By hilling we mean drawing soil up against the base of the plants. We use a garden hoe to do this. Hilling soil against the plants will keep any potato tubers from turning green due to exposure to sunlight. Another technique is to place a 6-inch layer of straw mulch around the plants as they develop. This technique makes harvesting potatoes quite easy.

**Apply neem (a botanical insecticide) to control flea beetles** on young plants of cabbage and related crops. These tiny beetles are about 1/16 inch long and are named for their habit of jumping like fleas when disturbed. They chew holes in plant leaves and can severely retard the growth of many vegetable crops.

**Don't apply mulches for weed control just yet.** The ground is still a little too cool for that. Wait until soil temperature reaches 60°F (15°C) before applying mulches around vegetables.

## Harvest

**Harvest asparagus spears.** Resist the temptation to harvest asparagus in the first year of planting. When harvesting from beds 2 years or older, cut or snap off the spears at ground level. Don't leave aboveground stubs. These tender stubs may attract asparagus beetles or provide an entry point for disease. The tough, fibrous underground stems eventually dry and shrivel after the harvest.

# 1 week before average date of last frost

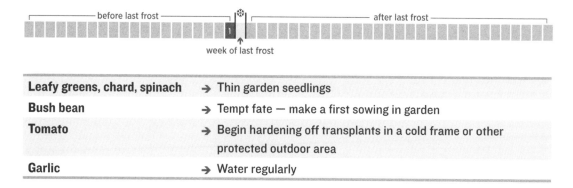

before last frost — | ❄ | — after last frost

**1**

↑
week of last frost

| | |
|---|---|
| **Leafy greens, chard, spinach** | ➔ Thin garden seedlings |
| **Bush bean** | ➔ Tempt fate — make a first sowing in garden |
| **Tomato** | ➔ Begin hardening off transplants in a cold frame or other protected outdoor area |
| **Garlic** | ➔ Water regularly |

## Seeding and Planting

**Tempt fate by making the first sowing of bush green beans.** Jack Frost may pay a visit, but it's worth the risk to try an early sowing. Save plenty of beans for later plantings, just in case. Plan to make additional sowings at 10- to 14-day intervals through mid-summer.

**Begin hardening off tomato plants,** but avoid exposing seedlings to temperatures much below 60°F. Do not harden off seedlings of other warm-season crops, though, because hardening off slows growth enough in peppers, eggplants, and squash that you may end up with reduced yields of vegetables.

**Soak soil the day before transplanting vegetable seedlings.** Also, water seedlings in their containers a few hours ahead of planting. Never plant in dry soil. Plant in late evening when air is cool and humid. This prevents seedlings from wilting and gives them some stress-free time to recover from transplanting.

## Maintenance

**Thin plantings of leafy greens** such as chard and spinach, but don't throw away the small plants. Thinned-out seedlings are perfectly edible. Of course, it will take a lot of thinned seedlings to get enough for a meal. That's why we're not fussy about the spacing of seed when sowing greens. Not having to be meticulous is a great relief.

**Water garlic regularly** through late July, unless rainfall is frequent. Garlic bulbs will be small if grown under dry conditions. An application of high-nitrogen fertilizer such as dried cow manure when garlic plants are about 6 to 8 inches tall will also help promote large bulb development.

*Save the thinned seedlings of leafy greens to incorporate into salads.*

# Last frost to 2 weeks after last frost

### Dates in my area:_____ to _____

## SEED STARTING

- Cucumber, squash, melon → Try early sowing in garden
- Sweet corn → Make first sowing
- Nasturtium → Sow among vegetables or in spare corner of garden
- Anise, chervil, cilantro, dill → Sow seed directly in garden or transplant seedlings started indoors
- Okra → Sow seed in garden
- Bush green bean → Make second sowing in garden
- Pole bean → Sow seed next to trellis or poles
- Summer savory → Sow seed near bush bean plantings
- Leaf lettuce, carrot, beet, sweet corn, radish → Make additional sowings in garden
- Bush-type summer squash → Sow seed for container planting
- New Zealand spinach → Direct-sow in garden

## PLANTING

- Basil → Set out plants in the vegetable garden, keep a pot near the kitchen door
- Cucumber, squash, melon → Set out transplants
- Tomato, pepper, eggplant → Set out transplants

## MAINTENANCE

- General → Mow weeds around edges of garden
- All crops
  → Use stem collars to protect seedlings from cutworms
  → Check frequently for insect pests — e.g., aphids, flea beetles, tortoise beetles
  → Protect from slugs
- Broccoli, kale, cabbage, Brussels sprouts, kohlrabi, cauliflower → Check for imported cabbage butterfly larvae (green "worms")
- Strawberry
  → Pinch off blossoms on new plants
  → Mulch around plants to keep fruit off the ground
- Tomato, pepper, eggplant
  → Place mulch around plants
  → Place bamboo stakes next to eggplant and pepper transplants
- Potato → Hill plants again

## HARVEST

- Rhubarb → Continue harvesting
- Mustard greens → Harvest leaves
- Garlic → Cut scapes and use in cooking

YEAR_____

_____
_____
_____
_____
_____
_____
_____
_____

YEAR_____

_____
_____
_____
_____
_____
_____
_____
_____

YEAR_____

_____
_____
_____
_____
_____
_____
_____
_____

# week of average date of last frost

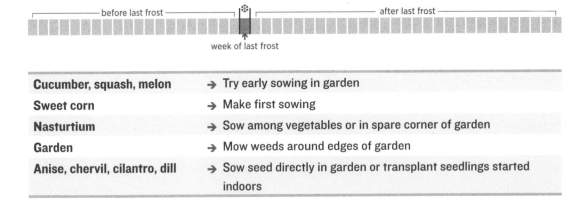

before last frost ─────── ❄ ─────── after last frost

week of last frost

| Cucumber, squash, melon | → Try early sowing in garden |
| Sweet corn | → Make first sowing |
| Nasturtium | → Sow among vegetables or in spare corner of garden |
| Garden | → Mow weeds around edges of garden |
| Anise, chervil, cilantro, dill | → Sow seed directly in garden or transplant seedlings started indoors |

## Seeding and Planting

**Begin sowing sweet corn.** Corn is wind pollinated, so plant seeds in blocks of at least four rows to ensure good pollen dispersal. Use floating row covers over seeds to keep away hungry birds and to warm soil for this heat-loving crop.

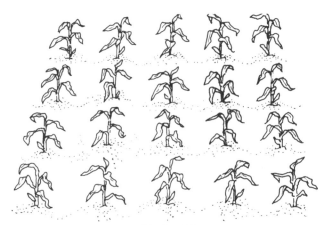

*Sow seeds of sweet corn in blocks of four or more rows to ensure good pollination.*

**Plant some nasturtiums among garden vegetables.** Nasturtium is not a very demanding plant and will thrive in less-fertile soils. Organic gardeners claim nasturtium repels whiteflies from crops such as tomatoes. Supposedly, they also attract aphids away from other crops. Even if they don't do either of these things, nasturtium flowers can be used to dress up salads.

**Sow seed of cucumber, squash, and melon** directly into the garden and cover the seeded area with floating row covers. Otherwise, wait until soil temperature warms to at least 60°F (15°C). One technique we use for early seeding is older than Methuselah. After sowing cucumbers and squash, typically two seeds at a time, we'll place a clear glass jar over the spot. The glass jar acts as a mini-greenhouse, warming soil and protecting emerging seedlings from cold. The glass will have to come off once seedlings are up a bit. Only one seedling will be allowed to get on with its life; the weaker of the two will be cut off with scissors. Yes, even in the garden, only the fittest survive.

Sow seeds of anise, chervil, cilantro (coriander), and dill directly into the garden or transplant those that were started indoors. We grow cilantro and dill both in the garden and in pots. We allow some of the garden plants to flower and set seed; we collect the seeds to use as a seasoning or save them to start next year's plants. Our potted plants are grown only for their fresh leaves.

Get kids interested in the garden. One way to do this is to build a "twig tepee." Arrange long bamboo poles or tree limbs in the form of a tepee and plant scarlet runner beans or other pole beans at the base of the poles. The beans climb the poles and provide a neat enclosure for kids to play in. Kids may even want to eat the beans that are produced.

## Maintenance

Keep weeds around gardens mowed. Many types of weeds harbor garden pests. For example, pigweed and smartweed are home to the larvae of the European corn borer.

*A "twig tepee" made from bamboo poles or tree limbs, with pole beans planted at the base, will attract kids to the garden.*

# Planting Tomatoes

**Jen:** *For the most part, gardeners are a patient lot, but at this time of year most of us are champing at the bit to get on with planting tomatoes. It takes every fiber of my body to resist the temptation to plant.*

*Dad speaks from experience about the wisdom of waiting, because of what will probably become known as the "Year of the Disastrous Tomato Crop." We planted tomatoes at what has traditionally been a safe time, and twice our planting of 80-plus plants (we really like tomatoes) was hit by late frosts. These cold snaps happened 12 days after our average date of last frost.*

**Ron:** I no longer worry about our tomato plants losing growing time. Since our soils are wet and cool and the nights are still chilly, the plants will not grow much anyway. At this point, they're better off remaining in the comfort and protection of the cold frame.

Tomatoes do not set fruit at temperatures below 58°F (14°C), and until nighttime temperatures are consistently in the mid- to upper 50s, I will practice restraint, no matter how much it hurts.

# Edible Flowers

**Ron:** The first time I was served a salad that included flowers among the greens I hesitated a bit. The idea of eating flowers was new to me. It shouldn't have been: I've been eating and enjoying broccoli and cauliflower all my life, and those are nothing more than unopened flower buds. Part of the hesitation was due to my concern that the salad preparer lacked a fundamental knowledge of botany, specifically the part that deals with poisonous plants. I shouldn't have worried — the salad with nasturtium and borage flowers was . . . well, okay.

Despite the reservations of people like me, cuisines that include edible flowers have become quite fashionable. As such, some trendy gourmets have taken to growing plants with edible flowers in their gardens. If you're the trendy sort, do be careful in the selection of flowers. Not all are safe to eat. Among those that are edible are pansies, violets, calendulas, roses, lavender, hyssop, sage, thyme, borage, chives, and nasturtiums. Also keep in mind that pesticides should not be applied to any plants whose flowers are to be used in food recipes. It ruins the flavor of the salad as well as the functioning of your kidneys, nervous system, and other body parts.

Health-care practitioners have learned that many flowers are very nutritional, and some have antibiotic as well as other medicinal properties. You can expect to see a flood of information on the food and medicinal qualities of edible flowers in the next few years. Much of this information will be coming from China, where the study of edible flowers is particularly intense. Stir-fried violets, anyone?

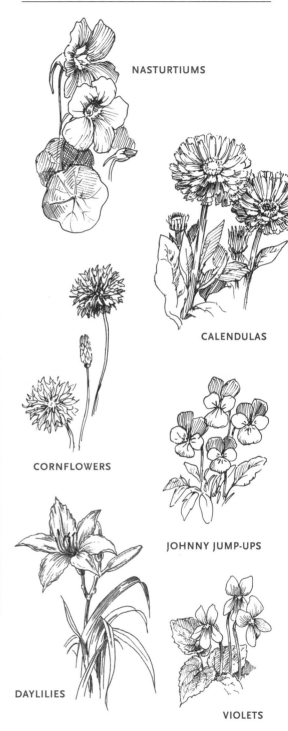

NASTURTIUMS

CALENDULAS

CORNFLOWERS

JOHNNY JUMP-UPS

DAYLILIES

VIOLETS

**Jen:** *Growing edible flowers is another great way to get kids involved in gardening. Just be sure they understand that it is okay to eat only the flowers you plant in the vegetable garden and when you're there with them. My son knows this rule by heart, although I'm careful not to grow poisonous ornamentals anywhere in the yard.*

*I've added nasturtium flowers to my green salads and tuna salads in the summer, much to the delight of my son, who says, "We're eating flowers, Mommy!" The flowers have a unique sweet and peppery flavor.*

*We also like to put "sugared" flowers on the tops of cakes we bake — we dip violet blossoms in water and then into cane sugar to coat the flowers. This really is "icing on the cake"!*

# 1 week after average date of last frost

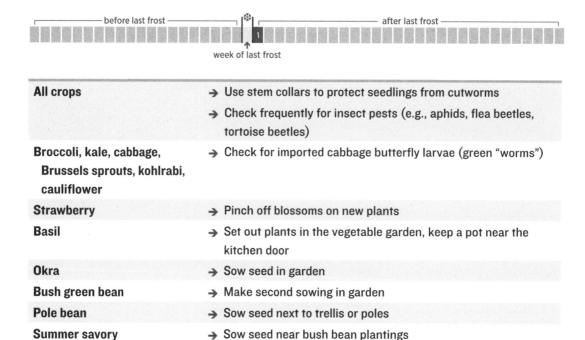

before last frost — ❄ — after last frost

↑
week of last frost

| All crops | → Use stem collars to protect seedlings from cutworms |
| | → Check frequently for insect pests (e.g., aphids, flea beetles, tortoise beetles) |
| Broccoli, kale, cabbage, Brussels sprouts, kohlrabi, cauliflower | → Check for imported cabbage butterfly larvae (green "worms") |
| Strawberry | → Pinch off blossoms on new plants |
| Basil | → Set out plants in the vegetable garden, keep a pot near the kitchen door |
| Okra | → Sow seed in garden |
| Bush green bean | → Make second sowing in garden |
| Pole bean | → Sow seed next to trellis or poles |
| Summer savory | → Sow seed near bush bean plantings |

*A gliding motion with a garden hoe is more effective than a chopping motion for ridding the garden of weeds.*

Use a gliding or slicing motion (rather than chopping) with a garden hoe to get rid of weeds. Our good friend the Ol' Admiral has always had difficulty mastering the workings of any piece of equipment that doesn't float. Just recently he admonished us for suggesting a gliding and slicing motion when using a hoe to remove weeds from the garden.

"It doesn't work," he grumbled. Then we reminded him that it was necessary to sharpen the hoe at least once in the lifetime of the tool. Landlubbers typically hone their hoes with a steel file several times during the gardening season (see illustration on page 36).

**Plan to share extra transplants with friends.** We always seem to have seedlings left over after transplanting tomatoes, peppers, and other crops. Sharing the extra plants is a great way to build friendships and encourage others to garden.

*Remove the flower spikes from basil to encourage more leafy growth.*

## Seeding and Planting

**Set out several plants of basil** in the vegetable garden if planning to harvest an abundance of leaves for making pesto. However, keep a pot of two or three basil plants near the kitchen. We use a couple of basil leaves almost every day when preparing meals. A few chopped leaves perk up a salad and round out the flavor of pasta sauces. Keep removing flower spikes from the plants as they appear to encourage more leafy growth.

**Sow okra seeds in light, sandy soil** and in the sunniest areas of your garden. Don't be put off by its reputation as a slimy vegetable. Okay, it's slimy, but it tastes great in soups and Creole dishes. Soak the seeds of okra for 24 hours before sowing them in the garden. When seeds come up, thin the plants to a spacing of 18 inches.

**Make a sowing of bush green beans and pole beans.** Pole beans involve a little more work than bush beans because of the need to construct some type of trellis or other support. Only one sowing of pole beans is needed since they yield continuously once they mature. On the other hand, bush-type beans grow faster and yield earlier. So we plant both: bush beans for early harvests and pole beans for later harvests. We have found that French haricot vert varieties such as 'Straight 'n' Narrow' yield over longer periods than other bush bean varieties.

**Sow seeds of summer savory near your green bean plantings.** This will help remind you to use savory leaves as a seasoning with cooked green beans.

## Maintenance

**Make weeding a priority in the garden now.** Many weeds are already setting seed, and it is critical to get these out of the garden before the seeds are dispersed.

A gardener we know was recently interviewed for a newspaper article on weeds. Our friend made the comment that "pulling weeds is a form of meditation." When the article appeared, it quoted her as saying that "pulling weeds is a form of medication." Some weeks, we do so much meditation in the garden that we think we'll need medication by the time we're finished.

**Protect seedlings from cutworms** by placing paper or plastic collars around stems of transplants. Cutworms are masters of stealth, chomping away on stems of plants through the night and then disappearing at daylight, leaving behind severed plants lying on top of the soil. You might be able to find the plump, gray larvae curled up just below the soil surface near plant stems. At that point, their fate is in your hands.

*Place paper or plastic collars around the stems of transplants to prevent damage by cutworms.*

**Pinch the blossoms from newly planted strawberries** (it hurts you more than it hurts them). The plants will be stronger and develop a better root system if not allowed to produce fruit this first year.

**Inspect vegetable crops every 3 or 4 days** for evidence of flea beetles, tortoise beetles, aphids, and other garden pests as well as plant diseases. This is the time

*Green cabbage worms will devour the leaves of cabbage, broccoli, and related crops if not controlled.*

of year when insect problems are beginning in earnest (in Massachusetts, in Ohio, in Maryland, in Kansas . . .). Early detection is key to good pest management. With early detection, many pests can be kept under control by simple handpicking or by using other mechanical methods such as traps (e.g., yellow sticky cards) and barriers (e.g., floating row covers, paper collars, screens).

**Look for little green visitors on cool-season vegetable crops** such as broccoli, kale, cabbage, Brussels sprouts, kohlrabi, and cauliflower. The green creatures are not aliens; they are cabbage worms. Actually, they are not worms but rather larvae of the imported cabbage butterfly. The adult white butterflies lay yellow eggs on the undersides of leaves. After hatching, the green larvae devour leaves and stems. Stave off infestations by covering plants with floating row covers to prevent egg-laying, or by squishing eggs and handpicking larvae while their numbers are small, or by spraying plants with *Bacillus thuringiensis* (Bt), a biological insecticide (sold under the brand names Dipel, Thuricide, and Safer's Caterpillar Attack). Add a few drops of spreader-sticker to the Bt before spraying. Spreader-sticker is sold at garden centers and helps Bt stick to waxy plant leaves.

# PROTECTING PLANTS FROM WIND

WINDS CAN DEVASTATE newly transplanted seedlings. Water lost through leaves of young plants — with the aid of strong wind — is not readily replaced because seedlings have yet to establish their root systems.

Covering transplants with row covers, bushel baskets, or milk crates can help prevent wind-related damage. Inserting cedar shakes or other pieces of thin wood into the ground next to plants can act as windbreaks and help protect seedlings.

*Place cedar shakes in ground next to vegetable transplants to protect them from the drying effects of strong winds.*

# 2 weeks after average date of last frost

before last frost ——————————————— ❄ | 2 —————— after last frost ———————————————

week of last frost

| | |
|---|---|
| **Tomato, pepper, eggplant** | → Set out transplants |
| | → Place mulch around plants |
| | → Place bamboo stakes next to eggplant and pepper transplants |
| **Cucumber, squash, melon** | → Set out transplants |
| **Strawberry** | → Mulch around plants to keep fruit off the ground |
| **All crops** | → Protect from slugs |
| **Potato** | → Hill plants again |
| **Leaf lettuce, carrot, beet, sweet corn, radish** | → Make additional sowings in garden |
| **Bush-type summer squash** | → Sow seed for container planting |
| **New Zealand spinach** | → Direct-sow in garden |
| **Rhubarb** | → Continue harvesting |
| **Mustard greens** | → Harvest leaves |
| **Garlic** | → Cut scapes and use in cooking |

## Seeding and Planting

**Set out transplants** of tomato, eggplant, cucumber, squash, and melon. Conditions should be ideal for the successful establishment of these plants. If possible, transplant on a cloudy day just before a rain. Spindly tomato plants may be planted deep since they are capable of forming roots all along their stems. (See To Stake or Not to Stake page 100, for methods of growing tomatoes.)

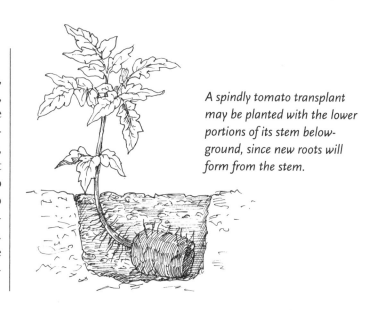

*A spindly tomato transplant may be planted with the lower portions of its stem below-ground, since new roots will form from the stem.*

Peppers like it hot but leaf lettuce does not. To keep lettuce growing during the hot days of summer, we shade the plants and keep them well watered.

**Set out pepper plants.** There isn't much to be gained with earlier planting of peppers if nights have been cool. Peppers are of tropical origin and they like it hot. In fact, their flowers will usually fall off when nighttime temperatures are below 60°F (15°C).

Transplant pepper seedlings in soil a little deeper than the pot or flat they grew in. Studies show that deeper-planted peppers produce higher yields than those at normal depths. Also, the plants are less likely to fall over later in the season when weighed down with fruit.

**Place a bamboo stake next to eggplant and pepper seedlings** as you transplant them or soon thereafter. Eggplant and peppers often get top heavy when loaded with large fruits, and as a result, plants will often topple. We tie the

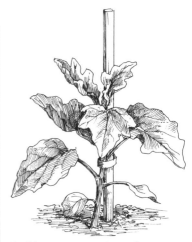

*Staking pepper and eggplants will keep them from toppling over when weighed down with fruit.*

plant stems to the stakes when the plants get tall enough.

**Continue with successive seeding** of leaf lettuce, carrots, beets, sweet corn, and radishes. Provide some shade for new plantings of leaf lettuce. Leaf lettuces can be planted throughout the growing

## EGGPLANT, A SUPERFOOD

WE MENTION EGGPLANT as one of the warm-season crops for our gardens, but frankly not a lot of people seem to be growing it. We admit that we haven't been too fond of this vegetable in the past, but some recent news has caused us to change our minds.

Scientists at the Agriculture Research Service of the U.S. Department of Agriculture report finding uniquely high levels of chlorogenic acid. Though that sounds like something one would use to disinfect a latrine, it is actually one of the most powerful antioxidants produced in plants. Antioxidants are chemical compounds that combat cancer-causing agents. Okay, add eggplant to our shopping list!

season but do best when shaded during the hot months of summer. Shade cloth can be used, but we prefer lattice for lettuce. Lattice is supported above the planting of lettuce by short-legged sawhorses, cement blocks, or crates. Keep lettuce well watered to prevent it from becoming bitter tasting.

**Sow seed of bush-type summer squash in patio containers.** 'Peter Pan' scallop squash, for example, is especially well suited for containers because its compact, bushlike form takes up little space. We like to harvest scallop squash when the fruits are no more than 2 inches across, and steam them whole. Tossed in olive oil or butter with fresh herbs, mini scallop squash makes a tasty alternative to sliced yellow or zucchini squash.

*Summer squash such as scallop squash grows well in a container on the patio or deck.*

# GARLIC SCAPES

THE HEALTH BENEFITS of garlic are frequently ballyhooed in the popular press; recently, we read an article stating that garlic helps reduce high blood pressure and also preserves youthful complexions. The first benefit has been pretty well documented in scientific literature, but we're not so sure about the latter effect.

Perhaps in response to its health-promoting effects, more and more gardeners are growing garlic. Most new garlic growers realize that the bulbs will be ready for harvest when plant tops have begun to turn yellow or brown. However, we'd guess that few appreciate the special treat awaiting them right now.

Hardneck varieties of garlic have begun sending up their so-called flower stalks or scapes. We say "so-called flower" stalks because garden-variety garlic plants do not flower but instead send up a stalk that eventually produces small bulblets at the tip. These bulblets, by the way, can be eaten or you can plant them in fall.

As a scape first elongates, it forms a curl. Later the scape straightens and toughens. In the curled stage, scapes are tender and have a subtle garlic flavor without the bite of mature garlic cloves. When cut from plants, garlic scapes can be sautéed, steamed, or chopped for salads, egg dishes, and stir-fries. We also use the scapes as a base in making a robust vegetable stock.

Nowadays, many vegetable growers are selling garlic scapes at farmers' markets. A few years ago most growers cut the scapes — to promote better garlic bulb development — and left them in the field to rot. Times have changed; garlic scapes are now considered a gourmet delight.

*Harvest garlic scapes when they begin to curl. Use them in dishes that benefit from a light touch of garlic flavor.*

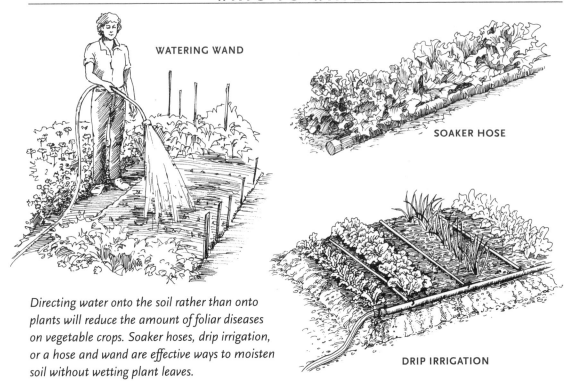

WATERING WAND

SOAKER HOSE

DRIP IRRIGATION

*Directing water onto the soil rather than onto plants will reduce the amount of foliar diseases on vegetable crops. Soaker hoses, drip irrigation, or a hose and wand are effective ways to moisten soil without wetting plant leaves.*

**Plant New Zealand spinach,** for a spinachlike harvest through the hot summer. It is not a true spinach but rather a warm-season crop that gets to be 2 feet tall or more with a spreading, branching growth habit. It is high in vitamins A and C and iron. Both leaves and stems can be used in recipes that call for spinach.

## Maintenance

**Lay mulch around tomato, eggplant, and pepper plants.** We use straw, but another option we are considering is reflective mulch. Researchers at the University of California and at the University of Maine demonstrated that plants growing over reflective mulch produce significantly higher yields than those without the mulch. Building paper with a foil surface works as a reflective mulch, but reflective plastic mulches are also available. Local garden centers may have these products. If not, check for sources on the Internet (see Resources, page 185).

**Direct water onto soil** around plants when watering garden vegetables. Avoid overhead watering of crops. Using sprinklers wets the leaves of vegetables and may promote leaf blights and mildew. Soaker hoses or drip irrigation systems moisten soil without wetting plant leaves. If you must use sprinklers to water the garden, turn them on early in the day, rather than in the evening, to enable leaf surfaces to dry during the day.

**Place a mulch of salt hay, straw, or pine needles around strawberry plants.** This will keep ripening fruit from turning to strawberry jam as a result of contact with wet ground.

**Protect plants from slugs.** If it's been raining frequently, slugs are likely taking their toll on emerging seedlings in your vegetable garden. There are a lot of ways to control slugs, including the infamous beer-trap technique. Not wanting to waste a good beer, we sometimes scatter sharp sand, crushed clamshells, or eggshells near susceptible crops. Also, frequent cultivation will dry soil and deter slugs. They like it wet. (See Scourge of the Slugs, page 123, for more methods of slug control.)

**Be careful when cultivating around garden peas.** Peas have shallow roots that are easily damaged. We put a light layer of straw mulch around peas to protect them from our heavy-handed cultivation technique and to keep weeds down and soil moisture high. The mulch will also keep the ground cool, something pea roots appreciate.

*Control Colorado potato beetles by handpicking the adult beetles and by crushing their orange-colored egg clusters found on the undersides of potato leaves.*

**Hill potatoes for the second time this season.** Also, remove and destroy pesky striped Colorado potato beetles and their orange egg clusters (found on undersides of leaves).

## Harvest

**Continue harvesting rhubarb stalks.** Any surplus rhubarb stalks we have are cut into 1-inch pieces, placed in freezer bags, and then tossed into the freezer. No blanching is necessary.

**Begin harvesting mustard greens** when plants reach a height of 6 to 8 inches. Typically, harvest begins about 5 to 6 weeks after seed is sown. We snip off the outer leaves and leave intact the center (or crown) of each plant, so it will continue to yield tender and mild-flavored leaves. Once hot weather arrives, the leaves tend to become too pungent for those with a tender tongue or a sensitive digestive tract.

**Cut off and use the flowering stalks from garlic plants.** Removing the stalks (called scapes) encourages larger bulb growth. (See Garlic Scapes, page 97.)

## CULTIVATION

THIS IS A TRANSITION TIME IN THE GARDEN. Though planting continues, our attention shifts more toward maintenance activities: watering, weeding, thinning, mulching, pinching, pruning, and cultivating.

Maybe the least understood of these tasks is cultivation. Many gardeners cultivate because "it makes the garden look nice." That's a good reason for cultivation, but the real purpose goes a little deeper.

After initial soil preparation and planting, soils begin to get compacted from pounding rainfall and foot traffic; also, the soil surface can develop a crust as it bakes in the summer sun. By cultivating with a hoe, rake, or other tool, we break the crust and relieve soil compaction, enabling better movement of air into the soil. Oxygen in air is essential for plant root development and for the survival of the many organisms in soil that contribute to the health of plants and fertility of soil. Cultivating also allows rainwater to penetrate soil rather than run off the surface.

# TO STAKE OR NOT TO STAKE

OF ALL THE VEGETABLES IN THE GARDEN, perhaps none has more methods for growing than tomatoes. They may be allowed to sprawl over the ground, tied to stakes, trained to a trellis, or grown in cages or in hanging baskets. Each method has its advantages and disadvantages.

**SPRAWLING.** This is the easiest and least labor-intensive method for growing tomatoes. The tomato seedling is planted in the ground and then allowed to grow as a bushy but sprawling plant. It is a space-consuming way to grow tomatoes, but tomato plants grown this way produce the largest number of fruit. However, the fruit ripens later than those on plants grown by other methods. Also, the fruits are often in contact with the ground; this increases the chances for fruit rots and damage by slugs and snails. A mulch applied on the ground under the plants will reduce the risks of disease.

**STAKING.** With this method, one or two stems of the tomato plant are loosely tied to a stake that has been hammered into the ground next to the plant. Through the growing season, side branches and any new stems (called suckers) starting near the base of the plant are pinched off. Tomatoes produced on staked plants tend to ripen sooner and are larger than those grown by other methods. That's the good news. On the downside, you can expect fewer tomatoes per plant because most of the stems have been removed. That may not be a big deal since spacing between staked plants is less than spacing between unstaked plants — 18 inches versus 24 to 36 inches, respectively. Staking is stressful to tomato plants. Staked plants are often more prone to certain diseases.

**TRAINING TO A TRELLIS.** This method is similar to staking. A trellis is set up by stretching a strand of wire between 5-foot-high posts. Pieces of heavy twine are tied around the base of each plant and to the wire above the plant. Plants are spaced 18 inches apart, and each is pruned to one main stem. As the stem grows, the twine is carefully twisted around it. The pros and cons of this method are the same as for staking.

**CAGING.** An assortment of commercially produced cages for growing tomatoes is available at garden centers or from mail-order companies, but we found the best and most cost-effective cage to be one made from concrete-reinforcing wire (sold at building supply stores). Five-foot-long sections of the wire are cut and formed into cylinders 18 inches in diameter. The cylinders or cages are placed around the plants, which are spaced 2 feet apart. This is our favorite method of growing tomatoes. No pruning is necessary, plants are off the ground, and the fruit is easy to pick. As with sprawling tomatoes, the fruit ripens later but the yields are higher than for staked or trellis-grown plants.

**HANGING BASKETS.** Growing tomatoes in hanging baskets, right-side up, upside down, sideways, or any which way, can be useful for those with minimum garden space. The baskets can be hung from porch rafters, from hangers attached to sides of buildings, or from tall in-ground posts. The key to success with this method of growing is to use dwarf or patio-type tomatoes that have a compact, bushy growth habit and thick stems. There will be less stem breakage than with tall-growing tomato varieties. Also, be aware that tomatoes grown in hanging baskets will need more frequent watering than will those grown in the garden.

HANGING BASKET

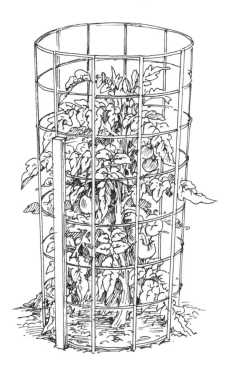

CAGING

STAKING

# 3–5 weeks after average date of last frost

Dates in my area:_____ to _____

## SEED STARTING

| | |
|---|---|
| ▪ Brussels sprouts, cauliflower, cabbage, broccoli | → Sow seed in pots, flats, garden for late-season harvest |
| ▪ Rutabaga | → Sow seed in garden |
| ▪ Bean, squash, sweet corn | → Resow if first sowing failed |
| ▪ Bush green bean | → Make another sowing in the garden |
| ▪ Summer squash, bean, carrot, fall cabbage, turnip, leaf lettuce | → Sow seed in areas vacated by early crops |
| ▪ Escarole, endive | → Sow seed for fall harvest |

## MAINTENANCE

| | |
|---|---|
| ▪ Most crops | → Mulch around plants |
| | → Side-dress plants with all-purpose natural fertilizer |
| ▪ Garlic | → Place straw mulch around plants to keep soil cool and aid bulb development |
| ▪ Herbs | → Do not mulch plants |
| | → Check for four-lined plant bug damage |
| ▪ Potato | → Handpick potato beetles, if present |
| ▪ Cabbage, cauliflower, broccoli, kale | → Keep monitoring for cabbage worms |
| ▪ Tomato | → Check for whiteflies |
| ▪ Leek | → Hill soil around stems |
| ▪ Onion, shallot, leek, garlic | → Weed regularly |
| ▪ Strawberry | → Remove all but two or three runners from new plants |
| ▪ Summer squash | → Protect from squash vine borer |
| ▪ Corn | → Control corn borer with Bt |

## HARVEST

| | |
|---|---|
| ▪ Strawberry | → Harvest daily |
| ▪ Asparagus | → Continue harvesting spears |
| ▪ Leaf lettuce | → Harvest |
| ▪ Carrot | → Harvest baby carrots |
| ▪ Parsley | → Harvest outer leaves |
| ▪ Basil | → Harvest leaves |
| ▪ Snow pea | → Harvest while pods are flat |
| | → Cut some tendrils for use in cooking |

YEAR_____

YEAR_____

YEAR_____

# 3 weeks after average date of last frost

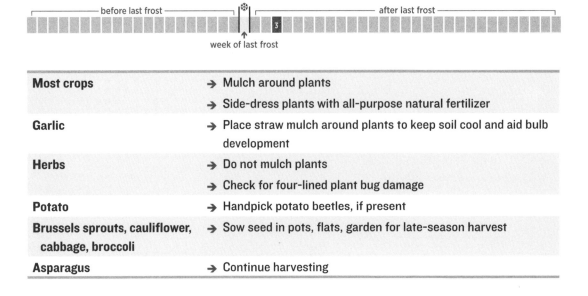

before last frost — ❄ — after last frost

week of last frost

| Most crops | → Mulch around plants |
| | → Side-dress plants with all-purpose natural fertilizer |
| Garlic | → Place straw mulch around plants to keep soil cool and aid bulb development |
| Herbs | → Do not mulch plants |
| | → Check for four-lined plant bug damage |
| Potato | → Handpick potato beetles, if present |
| Brussels sprouts, cauliflower, cabbage, broccoli | → Sow seed in pots, flats, garden for late-season harvest |
| Asparagus | → Continue harvesting |

## Seeding and Planting

Sow seed of cabbage, cauliflower, and broccoli for late-season harvests. Start the seeds in pots, flats, or small garden beds. Seedlings will be ready for transplanting in 4 to 6 weeks to areas of the garden vacated by early-season crops such as peas.

Sow seed of Brussels sprouts for a fall crop. Brussels sprouts started now will be more productive and better tasting than Brussels sprouts started in early spring. Summer-harvested sprouts are too bitter for our tastes. Seeding may be done in flats or in a small bed in the garden.

## Maintenance

Apply mulch around most vegetable crops. If soil is dry, water it before you apply mulches. Mulches keep soil moist and cool during hot, dry weather; retard growth of weeds; and prevent soil from splashing onto plant leaves. It's not just a matter of keeping leaves looking clean — soil often carries soilborne plant diseases. A clean plant is a healthy plant. Straw mulch is our favorite but is sometimes difficult to find. Salt-marsh hay is popular but more expensive than straw. Spoiled hay is quite common but has many weed seeds.

Place straw mulch around garlic plants. Garlic bulbs don't develop well when soil temperatures exceed 68°F (20°C), so mulch will keep soil cool for good bulb development. Mulch also keeps the soil moist, another important factor in bulb development.

Don't mulch herbs. Most herbs prefer dry conditions. Mulches will keep soil too moist, and mulches around plant stems may cause stem rot. However, we will sometimes spread pea stone or gravel on the ground around perennial herbs, especially lavender. The stones keep water draining freely away from plant stems.

Gardeners in coastal areas sometimes use crushed oyster shells for the same effect.

**Side-dress vegetable crops with a general-purpose natural fertilizer.** No, side-dressing has nothing to do with a fashion statement. "To side-dress" means to apply fertilizer alongside crops in a row. We usually side-dress our crops twice during the growing season.

**Examine herbs for damage caused by the four-lined plant bug.** As its name implies, the adult bug has four black stripes down its yellow or green body. The nymph stage of this insect is reddish orange. Damage to plants appears as small, round, sunken spots on leaves and can be severe if plant bug populations are high. Covering plants with row covers will keep away the pest. For existing infestations, an application of natural pyrethrin may be necessary. Always read and follow

label directions when using any pesticide, including natural ones.

**Handpick Colorado potato beetles now,** before their population builds. Look for potato beetles and their larvae on eggplant as well as potato plants. If spraying is needed, find a biological product containing Bt (*Bacillus thuringiensis*) and labeled

specifically for Colorado potato beetle. Try the San Diego strain of Bt. This bacterial product is sold under the names M-One, M-Trak, Foil, and Trident. Apply Bt when the first brick red larvae, or "slugs," are visible on the plants. Continue applying Bt every 5 to 7 days, until no more larvae are observed.

## ALL THAT FLOWERS DOES NOT FRUIT

OH, HAPPY DAYS! When our tomatoes seem to be growing at a rate of about 2 inches per day and the plants are loaded with blossoms, that usually portends a very good yield of tomato fruit.

We say "usually" because an abundance of bloom does not necessarily guarantee an abundance of fruit. Flowering is followed by fruit set: that is, the initial development of the fruit that begins with pollination. With most tomato varieties, fruit set will not occur at temperatures below 58°F (14°C) or at temperatures above 85°F (29°C).

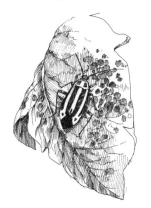

Four-lined plant bug is a common pest of basil, oregano, and many other herbs.

*Side-dress vegetable crops by applying fertilizer alongside crops in a row.*

# 4 weeks after average date of last frost

before last frost | week of last frost | 4 | after last frost

| Cabbage, cauliflower, broccoli, kale | → Keep monitoring for cabbage worms |
| Tomato | → Check for whiteflies |
| Leek | → Hill soil around stems |
| Onion, shallot, leek, garlic | → Weed regularly |
| Rutabaga | → Sow seed in garden |
| Bean, squash, sweet corn | → Resow if first sowing failed |
| Strawberry | → Harvest daily |
| Asparagus | → Continue harvesting spears |
| Leaf lettuce | → Harvest |
| Carrot | → Harvest baby carrots |

*Strips of old nylons or panty hose work well for tying tomato stems to stakes.*

Save old panty hose! Old nylons or panty hose are great for tying tomato stems to stakes. They are less likely to cut into and injure plant stems.

## Seeding and Planting

**Sow seed of rutabaga for fall harvest and storage.** Rutabaga, a cross between wild cabbage and turnip, stores very well.

**Make another sowing of beans, squash,** and other vegetables whose seeds may have rotted in the soil. Sometimes this is due to cool and wet weather, insect damage, or seeds being planted too deep.

## Maintenance

**Continue to look for cabbage worms** on cabbage, broccoli, cauliflower, and kale. Apply either Bt or the bacterial fermentation product spinosad to the plants for control.

**Shake the shoots of tomato plants.** If a large drift of little white things appears, it indicates an infestation of whiteflies on the plants. Whiteflies suck sap from the leaves of tomato and several other vegetable crops, causing leaf distortion and poor growth. Eventually the leaves turn yellow and drop. Weekly applications of insecticidal soap will limit damage from the flies. Be sure to get good coverage on the underside of leaves.

**Hill up soil around stems of leeks every few weeks.** Hilling is done to blanch the stems — that is, turn them white. Another way to blanch leeks is by placing stiff paper collars around shoots; the collars will keep soil and grit from getting between layers of leaf tissue. There's no particular time to harvest leeks, as they'll continue to grow right up to the time that the ground begins to freeze. We usually wait until stems are as thick as a thumb and then harvest them as we need them.

**Weed onions and their close relatives** (shallots, leeks, garlic) regularly. Onions do not like company, specifically the company of weeds. Onions have very shallow root systems and will starve if they have to compete with weeds for water and nutrients. Starving onions don't form very large bulbs, and who can blame them. So, we make it a point to weed our rows of onions frequently. Judging from their rapid rate of growth, they appreciate our efforts.

*Placing stiff paper collars around the stems of leeks is a cleaner alternative to blanching leeks by hilling soil around the stems.*

# BATTLE OF THE BEETLE!

THE BATTLE OF THE BEETLE is about to begin. No, it's not a demolition derby for Volkswagens; we're talking about Japanese beetles. They're emerging now and will feed on a wide variety of plants (about 300 different species — that's more than the most ardent vegetarian eats). They have great affection — and appetite — for our bean crop. We try to get a jump on the beetles before their population builds beyond our capacity to protect our beans. We handpick the first beetles that appear on the leaves of our beans and drop them into a bucket of soapy water. Apparently, they have an aversion to bathing. The best time to handpick Japanese beetles is early morning or late evening when, like most of us, they are lethargic.

We've tried Japanese beetle traps but find that these are so effective in attracting beetles that we get the neighbors' infestations as well as our own. Often the beetles pause to snack on our beans before entering the traps, so we don't use traps. Other options for control are applying a natural insecticide, such as neem oil or rotenone, and covering crops with floating row covers. When using any pesticide, whether or not it is natural, read and follow label directions.

*Control Japanese beetles by handpicking or by applying a natural insecticide to susceptible crops.*

## Harvest

**Pick strawberries daily,** preferably early in the day while they are still cool and firm. Strawberries ripen fast. Ripe fruit is very succulent and will rot quickly if not picked regularly, particularly in rainy weather. Freeze the excess harvest after washing the fruit and discarding any with soft spots or mold. Spread berries on a baking sheet, then place sheet in the freezer. When frozen, toss the berries into a freezer bag.

**Cut asparagus spears for a few more days,** then stop the harvest for this season. Let the remaining spears develop their fernlike shoots. Apply a high-nitrogen fertilizer to the asparagus bed and keep the plants watered well through the growing season to ensure a good harvest next spring. Among natural fertilizers that are high in nitrogen are blood meal, cottonseed meal, soybean meal, fish emulsion, and animal manures. Ammonium nitrate, potassium nitrate, and urea are synthetic sources. Check product labels for application rates.

**Harvest lettuce.** Leaf lettuce planted early in the season is ready to be picked. We suggest cutting some outer leaves or cutting all the leaves if plants are growing well, but don't pull up the plants. By not pulling up lettuce plants, they will continue to produce new leaves for some time. Use this technique with spinach, chard, and other leafy greens.

**Pick early-planted carrots as baby carrots now.** The same is true for other root crops such as turnips, scallions, radishes, and beets (though many people prefer to harvest beets as greens rather than as bulbous roots).

---

## THE ROOT OF RUTABAGA

THE ORIGIN of the funny-sounding word *rutabaga* is Swedish. It is derived from *rota bagge*, meaning "root ram," "baggy root," "thick root," or "ram's foot." Some other names for the cold-hardy vegetable are swede, Swedish turnip, neep, and yellow turnip. It grows best in northern climates, and we suggest planting it a few weeks after the frost-free date for a late-season harvest.

---

*Harvest leaf lettuce by cutting the outer leaves or all leaves, but leave the crown intact so that it can continue to produce new leaves.*

# KICK THE CAN!

TOO OFTEN when insects are spotted in the garden, many a vigilant gardener's first response is to reach for a can of insecticide and blast the critters. Though this is one option in pest management, a better approach is to use a number of strategies. These may be mechanical or cultural as well as chemical. However, the first step is to learn about insects inhabiting the garden. Not all insects are bad guys; some wear white hats.

Okay, no hats, but a number of predatory insects help control pest insects in the garden. Among these are parasitic wasps, ground beetles, lacewings, lady beetles, dragonflies, spined soldier bugs, and assassin bugs. Information and pictures of many beneficial insects can be found online and in various publications (see Resources, page 185).

Try to identify insects you see in the garden; learn about their life cycles, what they feed on, and a little about their behavior. This way, you can make wise and safe choices in controlling garden pests.

**LACEWING**

**LADY BEETLE**

**ASSASSIN BUG**

*Learn to identify beneficial insects in the garden. Because these insects prey on pests, they are an important part of any pest management strategy for gardeners. Three common beneficial insects are (left) the lacewing, (middle) the lady beetle, and (right) the assassin bug.*

# 5 weeks after average date of last frost

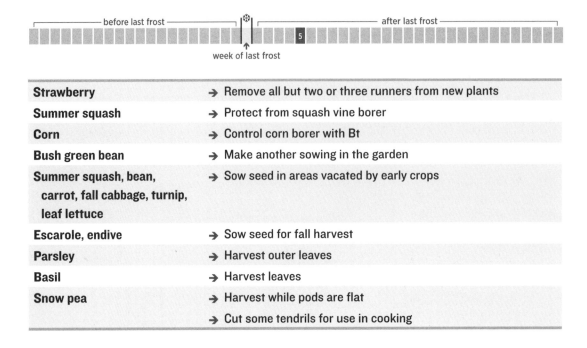

| Strawberry | → Remove all but two or three runners from new plants |
|---|---|
| Summer squash | → Protect from squash vine borer |
| Corn | → Control corn borer with Bt |
| Bush green bean | → Make another sowing in the garden |
| Summer squash, bean, carrot, fall cabbage, turnip, leaf lettuce | → Sow seed in areas vacated by early crops |
| Escarole, endive | → Sow seed for fall harvest |
| Parsley | → Harvest outer leaves |
| Basil | → Harvest leaves |
| Snow pea | → Harvest while pods are flat |
| | → Cut some tendrils for use in cooking |

## Seeding and Planting

**Make another planting of bush beans.** Most varieties of bush beans have a harvest period of only a few weeks at most, so for continuous yield, plant a succession of bush beans about every 2 weeks through midsummer.

**Plant escarole or endive as a leafy green.** Escarole and endive stand up well to summer heat and are not likely to bolt. They're actually the same species of plant, but endive has narrow, fringed or curly leaves, and escarole has broad leaves.

**Replant vacated areas from early crops** (such as radishes, spinach, and lettuce) with beans, summer squash, carrots, fall cabbage, turnips, and more lettuce.

## Maintenance

**Protect summer squash from squash vine borers** by applying rotenone or by placing row covers over the plants. The adult form of squash vine borer is a moth that closely resembles a bumblebee. A problem with using row covers to exclude insect pests is that they keep honeybees from pollinating the flowers. So, either the female squash flowers will have to be hand-pollinated by transferring pollen from male blossoms with an artist's paintbrush (see Maintenance, page 124) or row covers will have to be removed for several hours each day, and that may defeat the purpose of a row cover.

**Control corn earworm and European corn borer** by directing sprays of the biological insecticide *Bacillus thuringiensis* var. *kurstaki* into the silks of each ear of corn. Check the product label to be sure it contains this particular strain of Bt. Be aware that European corn borer is also fond of peppers. For best results, apply Bt about every 5 or 6 days until silks have dried — you'll have to make this summer's vacation a short one.

**Remove all but two or three runners (baby plants) from newly planted strawberries.** Replant runners you remove in another bed, or present them to a neighbor as a gesture of your generosity (or another way of saying "Keep out of my strawberry patch, Bucko!").

# VINEGAR AND CLOVE OIL AS WEED KILLERS

A WHILE AGO we received a free sample of a weed-killer product whose primary ingredients are clove oil and vinegar — not what we'd typically expect in an herbicide. The product reminded us of the initial testing of vinegar as a weed killer performed by researchers at the U.S. Department of Agriculture in Beltsville, Maryland, in 2001. They were able to kill 2-week-old seedlings of common weeds like lamb's-quarter, giant foxtail, velvetleaf, smooth pigweed, and Canada thistle by spraying the plants with 5 and 10 percent concentrations of vinegar. Household vinegar has a concentration of about 5 percent. Older plants of these weeds were killed with higher concentrations of vinegar.

In a more recent study, researchers at Penn State University compared the weed-killing efficacy of vinegar and clove oil. They found that both provided fair to good control of smooth pigweed, common lamb's-quarter, velvetleaf, and ragweed seedlings. The clove oil was as good as or better than vinegar in these studies.

The sample product we received contains both clove oil (8 percent) and vinegar (90 percent). Since this product is a general-purpose weed killer, you have to be very careful to avoid spray drifting onto vegetable crops. It just might put you in the mood to make some vinaigrette when you're finished harvesting, as well.

*Remove all but two or three well-spaced runners coming off the mother plants in the strawberry bed.*

*Young pea tendrils can be harvested and used in stir-fries, salads, and soups.*

## Harvest

**Harvest parsley as needed, but take only outer leaves.** Use scissors to cut off the outer fully developed leaves and let the central, younger leaves continue their development. Parsley is a good breath freshener; it's a good idea to stuff a pocket or two with a bunch of parsley when going out on the town tonight.

**Harvest some basil.** Use it in salads, as a seasoning in salad dressing, as a flavoring in herbal vinegar, as an ingredient in pasta sauces and other dishes, and for making pesto. With our daily harvesting of basil leaves, the plants never get a chance to bloom and, as a result, just keep producing more and more of their flavorful leaves. We ask a lot of our basil plants, and it helps their growth if we apply a dilute fertilizer solution every few weeks. (See The Basil Harvest, page 146, for information about making pesto.)

**Harvest snow peas while pods are still flat.** In contrast, sugar snap peas should be harvested when pods are plump. Pods of both of these types of peas are edible and great in stir-fries and salads.

**Cut some tendrils from pea vines.** Use the tendrils in salads and soups or in a vegetable stir-fry.

## KEEP IN MIND

DROP THE GYM MEMBERSHIP and work out in your garden! Gardening tasks get you fit. Mowing the grass around the garden with a push mower expends as much energy as engaging in aerobic exercises (and you don't have to wear spandex). Tilling the garden with a power tiller provides as much exercise, in terms of energy consumption, as does swimming over the same period of time. And weeding or cultivating the garden provides the same amount of exercise as golfing, with much less swearing.

# Sex and the Single Squash

**Ron:** There are the birds and the bees, and then there is zucchini. It seems that every year I'm called upon to give a lesson on the sex life of zucchini. Actually, that's a relief, since I don't know much about the intimate habits of birds and bees.

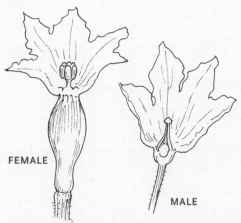

The teachable moment typically arises when someone complains to me that his or her zucchini plants are not yielding much fruit despite the appearance of numerous flowers on those plants. What this person does not realize is that the majority of blossoms seen are male flowers and as such do not produce fruit. Male and female flowers can be distinguished

*Squash plants have separate male and female flowers. Female flowers can be identified by the miniature squashlike structure just below the blossom. Male flowers lack this structure. Only female flowers produce squash fruit, but they require male blossoms for pollination.*

by examining their sex organs — pistils and stamens — but since this is a wholesome publication, I dare not go into detail. Suffice it to say that female flowers can be recognized by the miniature squash fruit just below the flower. Male blossoms lack this structure. This is true for all squash, gourds, pumpkins, melons, and cucumbers.

It is not unusual for summer squash to produce far more male than female blossoms. The ratio is about four male to one female blossom — not good odds for the guys. Furthermore, male flowers are much more common than female flowers early in the season, with a ratio of males to females as high as 15 to 1.

Add to this the fact that each male and female squash flower is open for 1 day only, and if pollination of the female flower does not occur (for example, if the weather is rainy for a long stretch and the bees aren't around), no fruit will develop. So, until the opening of male and female flowers is in sync, there'll be no hanky-panky in the squash patch and no wee little squash fruit.

I'm blushing! If you have any further questions about this topic, ask your parents.

# 6–8 weeks after average date of last frost

## Dates in your area: _____ to _____

### SEED STARTING

| | |
|---|---|
| ▪ Cilantro | → Make another sowing |
| ▪ Green bean, carrot, beet, kohl-rabi, turnip, chard, Chinese cabbage, and leaf lettuce | → Sow in vacant areas of garden |
| ▪ Mesclun | → Sow seeds in wide rows |

### PLANTING

| | |
|---|---|
| ▪ Warm-season cover crop | → Plant in unused areas of the garden |
| ▪ Brussels sprouts | → Transplant seedlings into garden |

### MAINTENANCE

| | |
|---|---|
| ▪ All crops | → Avoid working around plants when leaves are wet |
| ▪ Tomato | → Protect plants with a fungicide if symptoms of early blight appear |
| | → Remove suckers from plants tied to stakes |
| | → Place straw under plants to keep soil off leaves |
| | → Check for evidence of tomato hornworm |
| ▪ Squash, pumpkin, melon | → Spread straw under developing fruit |
| ▪ Swiss chard | → Cut off old, tattered leaves |
| ▪ Basil, rosemary | → Take shoot cuttings to start new plants |
| ▪ Strawberry | → Water once a week if weather is dry |
| ▪ Onion, garlic, shallot | → Apply nitrogen fertilizer |
| ▪ Summer squash | → Check plants for blossom blight |
| ▪ All squash | → Hand-pollinate to improve crop yield |
| ▪ Leek | → Hill plants again (at 2-week intervals) |

YEAR_____

_____

_____

_____

_____

_____

_____

_____

## HARVEST

| | |
|---|---|
| • Zucchini, summer squash | → Harvest when fruits are 3 to 4 inches long |
| • Shallot | → Harvest for use as scallion substitute |
| • English pea | → Harvest when pods are plump and firm |
| • Tarragon, basil, oregano, mint | → Harvest early in the day |
| • Broccoli | → Harvest large central heads |
| • Pickling cucumber | → Harvest when 2 to 6 inches long |
| • Tomato | → Harvest a few green tomatoes |
| • Potato | → Harvest some new potatoes |
| • Cabbage | → Harvest central head, but leave plant to form smaller side heads |
| • Green bean | → Harvest before pods bulge |
| • Radish | → Collect seedpods for use in cooking |

YEAR_____

YEAR_____

# 6 weeks after average date of last frost

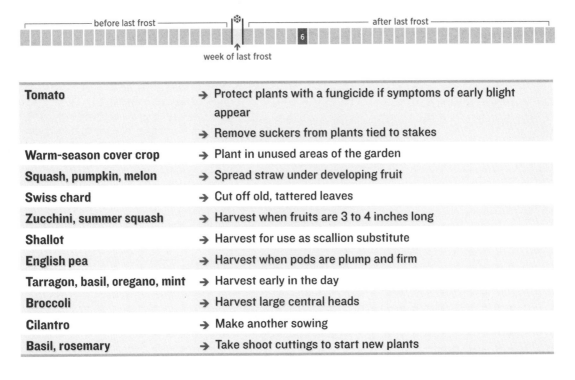

before last frost ——————— | ❄ | ——————— after last frost ———————

**6**

↑
week of last frost

| Tomato | → Protect plants with a fungicide if symptoms of early blight appear |
| | → Remove suckers from plants tied to stakes |
| **Warm-season cover crop** | → Plant in unused areas of the garden |
| **Squash, pumpkin, melon** | → Spread straw under developing fruit |
| **Swiss chard** | → Cut off old, tattered leaves |
| **Zucchini, summer squash** | → Harvest when fruits are 3 to 4 inches long |
| **Shallot** | → Harvest for use as scallion substitute |
| **English pea** | → Harvest when pods are plump and firm |
| **Tarragon, basil, oregano, mint** | → Harvest early in the day |
| **Broccoli** | → Harvest large central heads |
| **Cilantro** | → Make another sowing |
| **Basil, rosemary** | → Take shoot cuttings to start new plants |

## Seeding and Planting

**Plant a warm-season cover crop** of buckwheat, soybeans, or Sudan grass in open areas of the vegetable garden. Cover crops prevent soil erosion, conserve soil nutrients, and suppress weeds by shading soil. Shading discourages weed-seed germination.

**Make another sowing of cilantro (coriander).** Plants from the early sowing are now flowering and will soon set seed. Since we like to grow cilantro for its leaves, additional seed sowing through the season is necessary. Also, sow another crop of dill for its tender shoots. Let a few plants of cilantro and dill go to full maturity, as they will self-seed, giving a free crop next year.

**Take cuttings from nonflowering side shoots of basil plants.** Root these cuttings to create new plants to grow in pots on a sunny windowsill this winter.

**Take 2½-inch-long cuttings of rosemary and other woody herbs.** Strip off all leaves from the lower inch of each cutting. Then, dip the cut end in a rooting hormone (available at retail garden centers) and stick the cutting in a pot filled with a moistened mix of equal parts peat moss and coarse sand or perlite. Place a large, clear plastic bag over the pot; otherwise, be prepared to mist the cuttings with water each day until cuttings have rooted, in about 2 weeks. You'll know when the cuttings have rooted because there will be some resistance when they are gently tugged. An unrooted cutting will simply pull out of the rooting mix.

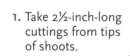

1. Take 2½-inch-long cuttings from tips of shoots.

2. Strip leaves from lower inch of each cutting.

3. Dip cut end in rooting hormone.

4. Stick cuttings in pots filled with a moistened mix of peat moss and sand.

## TOMATO TALES: BLOSSOM-END ROT

A COMMON PROBLEM that many tomato growers observe each summer is blossom-end rot, so called because the blossom end of tomato fruit (the end opposite the stem) develops a dark, sunken, leathery blotch.

The problem is not caused by any biological organism; it is a physiological problem. It is due to a deficiency of calcium in developing tomato fruit. Calcium deficiency typically occurs during periods of drought stress, or when there are drastic fluctuations in levels of soil moisture, or when tomato plants are over-stimulated with excess nitrogen-fertilizer applications. For reasons not completely understood, tomato plants that are heavily pruned — such as those that are staked — tend to be more susceptible to blossom-end rot than are unpruned plants.

Watering during dry periods, applying mulches around plants to maintain consistent levels of soil moisture, and using moderate levels of fertilizer will help prevent this problem. It is too late to do anything when tomato fruits are at or near their maturity.

*A dark, sunken, leathery blotch on the blossom end of tomatoes is symptomatic of a physiological disorder called blossom-end rot.*

*Early blight is a common disease of tomatoes. Symptoms first appear as dark, concentric-ringed spots on the lower leaves.*

## Maintenance

**Spray tomatoes with a copper- or sulfur-based fungicide** or a biological fungicide containing the bacterium *Bacillus subtilis* when the first symptoms of early blight are seen. Brown, concentric-ringed spots, appearing first on lower leaves, are the primary symptom of this disease. Early blight develops rapidly with hot, humid weather, so check plants every few days for symptoms. Fungicide applications should continue through the growing season at 7- to 10-day intervals. Whatever product is being used, be sure to read and follow the label instructions. The label is the law.

**Remove suckers from tomatoes that are tied to stakes.** In other words, remove new shoots that arise at the base of tomato plants and lateral shoots that appear in leaf crotches. (We don't bother removing suckers from tomatoes growing in cages or sprawling over the ground.) Keep in mind that staked tomatoes are somewhat stressed; it's not their natural habit of growth. That stress can contribute to the occurrence of blossom-end rot, a condition characterized by dry, sunken areas at the blossom end of tomato fruit. Keeping soil evenly moist with the help of regular watering, or with a layer of mulch, can help reduce the incidence of blossom-end rot.

**Place a deep layer of straw under developing fruit** of squash, pumpkins, and melons if using a sprinkler to water the garden or if rain showers become frequent. Straw will keep fruit from contacting wet soil and developing fruit-rot diseases.

**Cut off old, tattered leaves on Swiss chard.** The trimmed plants will soon send out tender new leaves. Swiss chard is a vegetable that can quickly outproduce your ambition to harvest it.

## Harvest

**Harvest zucchini and other summer squash** when fruits are 3 to 4 inches in length and while they still have the blossom attached. "Baby" squash have superior flavor to their older, bazooka-

*Regularly remove new shoots arising from the base of staked tomato plants and side shoots originating in leaf crotches. This is not necessary for tomatoes growing in cages or sprawling over the ground.*

size siblings. Harvesting summer squash while they are still small will encourage the parent plants to keep putting forth more fruit. Squash are not big on birth control.

**Harvest shallots to use as green onions.** Though we allow our main crop of shallots to fully mature, we don't hesitate to pull up a clump while they're still green whenever we have a need for scallions in a recipe.

**Harvest English peas when pods are plump and firm.** Pick peas as near to cooking time as is practical. Don't let picked peas sit around more than a day, since they rapidly lose their sweet flavor. Treat pea plants with kid gloves when harvesting the pods; their stems are very brittle and break easily when handled roughly. Peas will keep producing for several weeks as long as the plants are intact.

**Harvest shoots from tarragon, basil, oregano,** and other herbs early in the morning and when the weather is dry. Harvest even if you can't use the fresh herbs. Regular harvesting will keep herbs from flowering and keep them productive. Dry what can't be used fresh. Hang herbs to dry in a dark location to preserve their color and to minimize loss of essential oils. The oil content for basil, fennel, mint, sage, sweet marjoram, summer savory, and winter savory is highest just before their blossoms open, whereas that of rosemary and thyme is highest at full bloom.

**Put some pizzazz in your peas** by adding a few sprigs of mint to the cooking water. A few sprigs of mint leaves in your bathwater will put a little pizzazz in you, too.

**Harvest large central heads of broccoli plants** while heads are still firm and tight. Leave plants intact after removing the central head since they will continue to produce side shoots with small but tasty heads through the summer. The healthiest way to cook broccoli is by steaming. Spanish researchers found a significant loss of nutrients when broccoli was microwaved or boiled.

*Harvest the large central head (left) of broccoli while it is still firm and tight, but leave the plant intact since it will continue to produce small heads from side shoots (right).*

# 7 weeks after average date of last frost

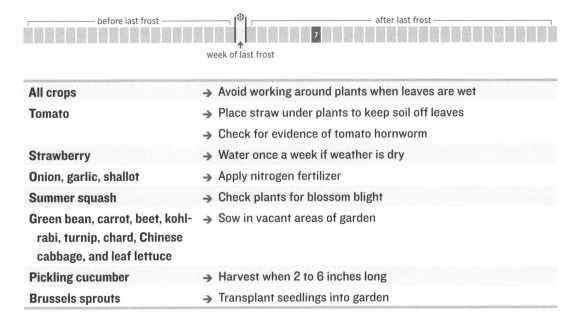

before last frost | week of last frost | after last frost

7

| All crops | → Avoid working around plants when leaves are wet |
| Tomato | → Place straw under plants to keep soil off leaves |
| | → Check for evidence of tomato hornworm |
| Strawberry | → Water once a week if weather is dry |
| Onion, garlic, shallot | → Apply nitrogen fertilizer |
| Summer squash | → Check plants for blossom blight |
| Green bean, carrot, beet, kohl-rabi, turnip, chard, Chinese cabbage, and leaf lettuce | → Sow in vacant areas of garden |
| Pickling cucumber | → Harvest when 2 to 6 inches long |
| Brussels sprouts | → Transplant seedlings into garden |

Avoid working around vegetable plants when their leaves are wet. Many diseases, such as bacterial blight of tomatoes and peppers and anthracnose of beans, are easily transferred from plant to plant as you make your way down the rows, brushing against plants.

Never use dog or cat poop, including kitty litter, in the vegetable garden. There is a risk to humans of catching certain animal diseases or parasites. Besides, the thought of pet poo scattered around vegetable crops doesn't do much for one's appetite.

Carry a pencil and this book when working in the garden. Those solitary moments when we're pinching, pulling, and plucking usually prompt thoughts of new plants for the garden or changes that need to be made. Also, discoveries are made in the garden every day — pests or diseases, but also recognition of beneficial animals and insects. If we didn't write down these thoughts, they would disappear irretrievably into the dimmest corners of our already dim minds.

## Seeding and Planting

Keep sowing vegetable crops in vacant areas of the garden. Green beans, carrots, beets, kohlrabi, turnips, chard, Chinese cabbage, and leaf lettuce can still be planted. If you have leftover seed, sow pea seeds for fall harvest. We don't always get a great fall crop of peas but the few we get are worth the effort. Incorporate some compost or organic fertilizer into the soil prior to sowing seeds, especially if sowing into a space where early-season crops were grown.

**Transplant seedlings of Brussels sprouts** that were started 4 weeks ago. Sprouts should be ready for harvest in about 90 days, ideally after some frosty weather.

## Maintenance

**Place straw under tomato plants** to keep water from splashing soil onto the leaves. Fungi causing certain foliar diseases on tomatoes live in soil. Watch for appearance of spots and yellowing on lower leaves of tomato plants. Promptly remove these leaves, but only when plant foliage is dry. The spots are symptomatic of disease, most likely septoria leaf spot or early blight, two common fungal diseases found on tomatoes at this time of year.

**Pull weeds when the weather is hot and sunny.** Weeds will wither quickly, and there's little chance that weeds left on top of dry soil will take root. Weed seeds brought to the surface during cultivation are less likely to germinate in dry soil. Now, if we can only get ourselves to weed the garden during the hottest part of the day. (See Garden Smart in Hot Weather, page 125, for precautions about gardening in the heat.)

**As harvest draws to a close, water strawberry plants** once a week if the weather is dry. This is the time when cell size of fruit buds is determined, and watering can dramatically increase next year's strawberry yield.

**Apply some nitrogen to onion, garlic, and shallot crops.** Use sodium nitrate, dried blood, cottonseed meal, or soybean meal. Apply no more than a small handful per 10 feet of row. A little nitrogen now will keep the plants greener for a while longer and result in larger bulbs.

However, too much nitrogen — and too much water — will result in bulbs that will not keep well in storage this winter.

**Water container gardens on a regular basis.** Keep in mind that vegetables planted in larger containers are better able to tolerate hot, drying winds and sun than those in smaller pots. Plants in small containers may have to be watered as often as three times a day to keep them from wilting. When applying water, be sure to saturate the soil.

*To prevent wilting, plants such as summer squash growing in a small container will have to be watered more frequently than one growing in a large pot.*

*Fuzzy growth at tips of young summer squash fruit
is a sign of blossom blight and leads to rotting of the fruit.*

**Check summer squash for blossom blight,** a fungus disease that infects the blossom, causing a white fuzzy growth, and then spreads into the fruit, causing a soft rot. Common under wet conditions, it can be controlled by improving air circulation around plants (removing excess foliage, keeping out weeds, or thinning overcrowded plants).

**Examine tomato plants carefully for evidence of tomato hornworm.** Signs of hornworm presence include stripped leaves and large dark granules of excrement. Though quite large, hornworms are not easy to locate because they are well camouflaged. When clues are present, start searching. Tomato hornworm is a green caterpillar with eight white V-shaped markings along each side. It feeds on the leaves and fruit of tomatoes. A close relative that also munches on tomato plants is the tobacco hornworm. It is similar but has seven diagonal white stripes along each side. Apply the bacterial insecticide Bt to plants as soon as caterpillars are found.

## Harvest

**Harvest pickling cucumbers** when they are 2 to 6 inches in length — that's about 5 days after blossoms open. Keep picking off little cukes regularly to promote more flowering and fruit production.

*Though it gets quite large, tomato hornworm can be difficult to find on tomato plants because it is so well camouflaged. Stripped leaves and large dark granules of excrement on and around plants are clues to the presence of hornworms.*

# SCOURGE OF THE SLUGS

LET'S SEE, one case of beer, two dozen pie pans, one dozen grapefruit . . . Hmmm, sounds like preparation for a wild party. In truth, those items are part of the arsenal we gather before engaging in battle with the slugs that have invaded every nook of our gardens. The slimy mollusks chew on cabbage, chard, lettuce, and the fruit and leaves of peppers, squash, and beans. And that's just the vegetables. Sadly, strawberries are another slug favorite.

Though there are enough control products on the market to make a slug quiver, we prefer methods that have worked for us in the past. For example, we use beer as bait to trap the brewski-loving critters. Our technique is simple. We sink pie tins or similar containers into the ground with top edges level with the soil. Then we sip some beer, pour some into the pan, sip some more beer, pour some into another pan, sip . . . and so on. Slugs can't resist the brew. The problem for them is that they have no self-control and soon drown their sorrows and their whole being in the beer.

Leftover grapefruit rinds also make good slug traps. We place grapefruit halves cutside down in various locations of the garden. Slugs like to hide under the grapefruit during the day. We surprise them as they slumber by picking up the grapefruit rinds and shaking the clinging slugs into a jar of soapy water.

This is not a happy time to be a slug, drunk, sober, or bathed.

*A pie tin sunk into the ground and filled with beer works well to attract, trap, and drown garden slugs.*

# 8 **weeks after** average date of last frost

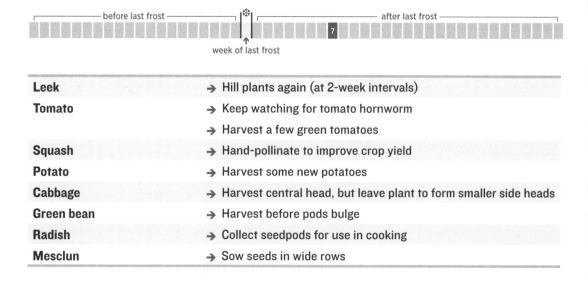

before last frost | week of last frost | after last frost

7

| Leek | → Hill plants again (at 2-week intervals) |
|------|------|
| Tomato | → Keep watching for tomato hornworm |
| | → Harvest a few green tomatoes |
| Squash | → Hand-pollinate to improve crop yield |
| Potato | → Harvest some new potatoes |
| Cabbage | → Harvest central head, but leave plant to form smaller side heads |
| Green bean | → Harvest before pods bulge |
| Radish | → Collect seedpods for use in cooking |
| Mesclun | → Sow seeds in wide rows |

## Seeding and Planting

**Sow seeds of leafy greens.** Buy a packet of mixed greens called mesclun. Some garden centers might still have racks of seed packets. Otherwise, create your own mix of leaf lettuce, endive, mustard greens, arugula, and any other seed remaining from earlier sowings of greens. Sow seeds using the wide-row method (see Well-Planned Planting, page 12).

## Maintenance

**Hill up soil around leeks again.** Continue to hill plants every 2 weeks.

**Keep examining tomato plants frequently for signs of tomato hornworm.** The caterpillars are still small now but can reach lengths of 4 inches when mature.

Occasionally, you may see a hornworm with a number of white projections on its top side. These are cocoons of a parasitic wasp. Leave a cocoon-loaded hornworm alone so that the wasp parasites can do their thing — kill the hornworm.

**Hand-pollinate squash plants** to improve crop yields in poorly performing beds. Use a small paintbrush to transfer pollen from male flowers to the sticky stigmas of female flowers.

**Use plain water to wash fruits and vegetables from the garden.** Some folks believe that bleach or soap should be used to do a thorough job of cleaning these foods. Not so! There is no evidence that bleach or soap will kill all or most

*Hornworm with cocoons of parasitic wasp on its back.*

of the bacteria on fruits and vegetables. Also, these materials usually leave residues that can make you sick. Just rinse produce under running water while gently rubbing the surface of the fruit or vegetable.

## Harvest

**Harvest some new potatoes.** A new potato is a small, immature tuber with skin so thin it doesn't need to be peeled, just washed. Harvest as needed by carefully scratching away soil at the base of plants. Use your hands. When you feel a potato, pull it out. Afterward, push soil back into place to cover those potatoes left for further development. Use new potatoes soon after harvest; they don't store well.

**Continue harvesting small, flavorful summer squash.** Their flavor is best preserved by steaming rather than boiling. Toss the squash with butter and chopped basil or another fresh herb. Summer squash grows fast; what is 3 inches long today will be 9 or 10 inches long in just another few days.

**Harvest a few green tomatoes** if you're getting impatient waiting for tomatoes to turn red. There are some great recipes for fried green tomatoes (see Resources, page 185). It might be a good idea to dig out Grandma's cookbook for other ideas on using green tomatoes.

*Harvest new potatoes by scratching away some soil from plants and digging out a few of the small tubers. Push back the soil and leave the plants intact to continue growing.*

## GARDEN SMART IN HOT WEATHER

SOME PEOPLE HAVE SAID that we don't know enough to come in out of the rain. We won't dispute that allegation, but for the record, we'll state that we know enough to come in out of the sun. The following precautions help us to avoid health hazards associated with hot, humid weather.

To start with, we drink plenty of water when gardening in the heat. We work on more-strenuous gardening activities early in the morning while it is still cool. Also, we take frequent breaks or stop gardening during the hottest time of the day. Our dress code includes a wide-brimmed hat; light-colored, loose-fitting clothing; sunglasses; and a liberal application of sunscreen.

Because we gardeners get so involved in our work, it's easy for heat stress to overtake us before we are aware of it. Thus, it's important to recognize the symptoms of heat stress and the more serious condition of heat stroke. Get information on heat-related illnesses at your doctor's office or see Resources on page 185 for a helpful Web site.

*small side heads of cabbage*

*bulging, overripe green bean (right) and proper-size bean (left)*

*radish seedpods*

**Harvest early cabbage** by cutting the head, but leave the plant and large outer leaves intact. Little heads of cabbage will develop at the base of the leaves later this summer and fall, perfect for a single serving of coleslaw.

**Harvest bush beans before pods bulge,** outlining the enclosed seeds. There's nothing chewier than pot-bellied green beans. If you're too late and your beans have begun to bulge, leave them on the plant and harvest as dry beans.

**Collect young seedpods of radishes that have gone to seed.** These are edible and taste great when steamed or used in stir-fries. Plus, they'll stimulate interesting conversation as dinner guests try to identify this strange new food.

# BATTLING TOMATO BLIGHT

HAPPINESS IS picking the first red tomato of summer. Sadness is seeing leaf spot and leaf blight diseases beginning to infect our tomato plants. At the moment, happiness and sadness are vying for control of our emotions. Early blight, late blight, septoria leaf spot, and an assortment of other fungal diseases are clearly visible in the form of spotted, yellowed, or browned leaves. Hot, humid weather accelerates the rate of infection by these diseases.

In the past, we haven't done much to control tomato diseases, except to hope that they'll develop slowly enough that our plants will still yield a decent amount of fruit before they expire. However, devastating crop losses in recent years have forced us into action beyond just hoping. We are using a bacterial product in anticipation of stifling further development of these diseases.

The product is quite unusual, though not new. It's a fungicide whose primary ingredient is *Bacillus subtilis,* a bacterium that occurs naturally in soil. It was first used by the German army in World War II to cure dysentery among its troops in North Africa. Later, scientists in England found that when applied to plant surfaces, the bacteria compete with disease-causing fungi for nutrients and space, and typically win the battle. The bacteria also release an antifungal chemical that has been shown to control powdery mildew, gray mold (botrytis), early blight, leaf spot, and many root pathogens.

# 9–11 weeks after average date of last frost

Dates in your area: _____ to _____

## SEED STARTING

| | |
|---|---|
| ▪ Spinach | → Sow in vacant areas for late harvest |
| ▪ Buckwheat | → Sow in vacant areas |
| ▪ Kale | → Sow seeds for late-season crop |
| ▪ Parsley | → Sow seeds in pots for indoor use |
| ▪ Leaf lettuce, root crops | → Make one last sowing |

## MAINTENANCE

| | |
|---|---|
| ▪ All crops | → Protect from Japanese beetles |
| ▪ Long-season crops (sweet corn, tomato, pepper, eggplant, winter squash, pumpkin) | → Side-dress plants with high-nitrogen natural fertilizer |
| ▪ Overripe or damaged fruit | → Remove to avoid attracting sap beetles |
| ▪ Squash, cucumber | → Check for striped cucumber beetles |
| ▪ Bean | → Check for Mexican bean beetles |
| ▪ Potato | → Keep picking Colorado potato beetles |
| ▪ Squash, melon | → Apply baking soda solution to powdery mildew |
| ▪ Carrot | → Maintain even moisture |
| ▪ Celery | → Blanch for a week before harvesting |
| ▪ Tomato, pepper, eggplant | → Control hornworms |
| ▪ Bean | → Continue to control Mexican bean beetle |
| ▪ Cabbage | → Twist heads to prevent splitting |
| ▪ Herbs | → Cut back to keep bushy |
| ▪ Cantaloupe, watermelon | → Avoid overwatering as fruit nears maturity |
| | → Pinch off late-season blossoms |
| ▪ Escarole, endive | → Tie outer leaves to blanch center leaves |
| ▪ Pea | → Turn under vines after harvest is over |

## HARVEST

| | |
|---|---|
| ▪ Continuously producing crops (e.g., cucumber, green bean) | → Harvest daily |
| ▪ Herbs | → Harvest leaves for drying |
| ▪ Pepper | → Harvest |
| ▪ Carrot | → Harvest small |
| ▪ Okra | → Harvest when pods are 3 inches long or smaller |
| ▪ Garlic, shallot | → Harvest when ready |
| ▪ Corn | → Harvest just before cooking |
| ▪ Summer squash, green bean | → Keep harvesting regularly |

YEAR_____

_____
_____
_____
_____
_____
_____
_____

YEAR_____

_____
_____
_____
_____
_____
_____
_____

YEAR_____

_____
_____
_____
_____
_____
_____
_____

# 9 weeks after average date of last frost

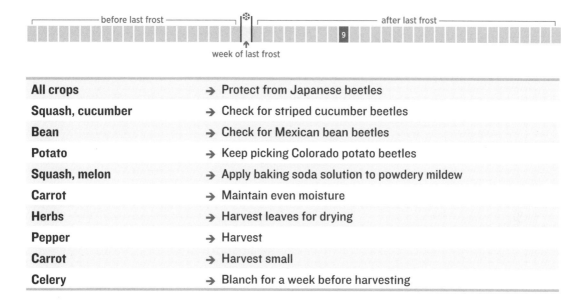

before last frost | week of last frost | after last frost | 9

| All crops | → Protect from Japanese beetles |
| Squash, cucumber | → Check for striped cucumber beetles |
| Bean | → Check for Mexican bean beetles |
| Potato | → Keep picking Colorado potato beetles |
| Squash, melon | → Apply baking soda solution to powdery mildew |
| Carrot | → Maintain even moisture |
| Herbs | → Harvest leaves for drying |
| Pepper | → Harvest |
| Carrot | → Harvest small |
| Celery | → Blanch for a week before harvesting |

## Maintenance

**Avoid heavy doses of nitrogen fertilizer** to tomatoes, peppers, and eggplant as a response to poor fruit set, especially if the plants are already growing well. Poor fruit set on these plants is most likely the result of cool nights (temperatures below 60°F [15°C]). Cool nighttime temperatures may also account for misshapen cucumbers.

**Keep after Japanese beetles.** Handpick when possible or apply a natural pesticide. If you do opt to use beetle traps, read the directions carefully. Many people mistakenly set traps in the middle of their flower or vegetable gardens.

Though traps effectively attract beetles, many of the critters stop to munch on garden plants before entering the traps. A better idea is to give the traps to neighbors who are upwind of your property. If they read the directions, they'll in turn give them to their upwind neighbors.

*Striped cucumber beetles not only chew holes in plant leaves but may also infect cucumber vines with a devastating bacterial wilt disease.*

**Look for striped cucumber beetles on leaves of squash and cucumbers.** It's bad enough that the beetles chew holes in young leaves of these plants, but the bigger concern is that cucumber beetles spread a bacterial disease that causes plants to wilt and then die. Once plants begin

¼"

to wilt, a sign of disease infection, the only recourse is to pull up and destroy the plants (by burying them). Apply one of the botanical pesticides, either rotenone or pyrethrum, to rid plants of the beetles. We have also hung yellow sticky traps (available at garden centers) just above our plants as a means of control.

**Check the underside of bean leaves for Mexican bean beetle,** a coppery brown-and-black-spotted beetle that looks much like a lady beetle. Unfortunately, the beetles are not there just waiting to do their famous Mexican bean dance. The adult beetles and their plump, yellow, spiny larvae feed on leaves of bean plants, often killing the plants. Handpick beetles and larvae or apply a pyrethroid type of insecticide

*Check the undersides of bean leaves for coppery, brown-and-black-spotted Mexican bean beetle adults and their yellow, spiny larvae.*

to bean plants, and crush yellow egg masses whenever they are found.

**Continue to handpick Colorado potato beetles** and their larvae from potatoes and eggplants. Drop the beetles into a jar of soapy water. Also, crush the orange egg masses that appear on the undersides of leaves.

**Apply a solution of baking soda** (sodium bicarbonate) to leaves of squash and melon plants at the first signs of powdery mildew. Make the spray solution by dissolving 1 teaspoon of baking soda in 1 quart of water. Another option for powdery-mildew control is to apply an ultrafine horticultural oil. Read the label directions before using any horticultural oil.

**Maintain even moisture around carrot plants.** Exposure to alternating dry and wet spells will

result in carrots with splits and cracks. Also water cucumber and tomato plants consistently; uneven watering may cause cucumbers to taste bitter and can contribute to blossom-end rot and splitting of tomatoes as they ripen.

**Withhold water from onions and potatoes** as their leaves begin to die. This helps harden bulbs and tubers in preparation for harvest and storage.

## Harvest

**Harvest leaves from basil,** oregano, dill, tarragon, and sage for drying. Freshly dried herbs taste much better than dried herbs that have sat in warehouses and on grocery shelves for months. The key to retaining the flavor of herbs is to dry them quickly. After a quick rinse in cold water to remove any grit, we spread herb leaves on trays in a food dehydrator, but they can also be air-dried. Dry culinary herbs in a dark but airy location. Good air movement hastens drying, as do

*Spread leaves of basil and other herbs on screens to air-dry.*

temperatures between 70 and 90°F (21 to 32°C). Once leaves are dried, store them whole in screwtop glass jars. Crush the herbs just before using them.

**Don't pull off old pea pods** that were overlooked during harvest. Leave pods on the plants, pull up whole plants, and hang them in a protected location for several weeks, until the pods are brown and thoroughly dry. Then shell the peas and use them for pea soup and other pea dishes.

**Harvest peppers as needed** — they'll stay crisper on the plant than in your refrigerator. Plan to leave some peppers on plants until the fruit turns red. All green peppers will turn red if given enough time.

**Use a garden spade to harvest carrots.** Pulling them by hand will often leave you holding a handful of leaves but no carrot. Push the spade into the ground about 4 inches away from the plants, and wedge carrots out. Most of the nutrients in carrots are located near the skin, so peeling carrots is not advised. Instead scrub the surface of carrots to remove soil. Also, some nutrients are lost as carrots dry. Store carrots in the vegetable drawer of the fridge to maintain their moisture.

*Pull up pea plants with overripe pods and hang them in an airy location to dry. When thoroughly dry, shell the peas and use in soups.*

**Blanch celery for about a week before harvesting** if you like tender and mild-flavored stalks. Blanching can be done by mounding soil around plants, wrapping leaf stalks with paper or aluminum foil, or placing boards against plants in the row. Blanch a few plants each week for a steady supply of tender celery. Leave a few plants unblanched; their stronger flavor will make them ideal for soups and stews.

*Remove the bottom from a coffee can and slip it over the plant when blanching celery.*

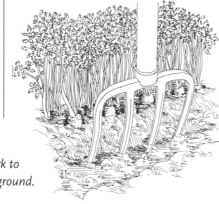

*Use a garden spade or fork to wedge carrots out of the ground.*

# 10 **weeks after** average date of last frost

before last frost | week of last frost | after last frost | 10

| | |
|---|---|
| **Tomato, pepper, eggplant** | → Control hornworms |
| **Bean** | → Continue to control Mexican bean beetles |
| **Cabbage** | → Twist heads to prevent splitting |
| **Okra** | → Harvest when pods are 3 inches long or smaller |
| **Garlic, shallot** | → Harvest when ready |
| **Continuously producing crops** (e.g., cucumber, green bean) | → Harvest daily |
| **Overripe or damaged fruit** | → Remove to avoid attracting sap beetles |
| **Spinach** | → Sow in vacant areas for late harvest |

Check out the dates and locations of agricultural fairs in your region. Unfortunately, there aren't as many fairs as there used to be, but it's still great fun to take the family to one.

## Seeding and Planting

**Sow seeds of spinach** in vacant areas of the vegetable garden for a fall harvest. Shade seedlings at least through midsummer and be sure they get plenty of water. Spinach needs 30 to 45 days from sowing to harvest, depending upon variety, so continue planting into early fall. 'Melody', 'Indian Summer', and 'Tyee' are good varieties for late-summer and fall planting.

## Maintenance

**Handpick hornworms** that are stripping leaves of tomato, pepper, and eggplant. Hornworms are too large now to control with biological products such as Bt, so handpicking is the best option for anyone not using synthetic pesticides.

**Grab a head of cabbage and give it a sharp twist.** This is not only a great way to take out your frustrations, but it will also prevent fully formed heads from splitting. By the way, don't try this on human heads. It really hurts.

**Remove all overripe or damaged fruit** from vegetable crops regularly to avoid attracting sap beetles. Sap beetles love to feed on damaged fruit. Usually they invade tomatoes that have

*Twist a head of cabbage to keep it from splitting.*

# Squash Vine Borer

**Ron:** All eyes were on me as I proceeded with the deftness of a skilled surgeon, carefully inserting the sharp knife through the epidermal layer. My assistant stood by to lend a hand; a good thing, since I needed someone to hold my beer as I worked feverishly to extract the infecting organism. As everyone watched, I was finally able to remove the life-threatening pest. All breathed a sigh of relief. This zucchini would live another day.

And that was how we spent one weekend, or part of it: surgically removing squash vine borers from our zucchini plants.

Sudden wilting of squash vines is the first symptom of borer invasion. A conclusive diagnosis can be made by inspecting the base of a vine for a hole that exudes wet sawdust–like frass.

Unfortunately, surgery is the only recourse once borers have invaded the stems of summer squash, winter squash, pumpkins, and gourds. To remove a borer, slit the stem lengthwise with a sharp knife until the borer is located. Remove the borer and then cover the stem with some soil just above the point of injury. With some luck, the stem will form new roots and the plant will continue to grow and produce squash fruit.

*Use a sharp knife to slit open a squash stem infected with squash vine borer. After removing the borer, cover the stem with soil.*

cracked or have been damaged by birds, slugs, or disease. Exposure of tips of corn ears by impatient gardeners and raccoons checking corn for ripeness also entices sap beetles.

## Harvest

**Be prepared to harvest vegetable crops daily.** Many crops are maturing rapidly and are best, as far as taste and nutrition are concerned, if they're picked before they become overripe. Like most gardeners, we find there are more vegetables ripening than we can eat in a day. So unless you can find willing recipients of the excess (keep in mind the needs of local food pantries when dealing with abundant harvests — see information on Plant a Row for the Hungry in Resources, on page 185), be prepared to can, freeze, or otherwise preserve what you can't eat immediately.

If you're not familiar with the techniques of preserving fruits and vegetables, talk to people who are canning enthusiasts or look for classes on food preservation offered by the Cooperative Extension or other organizations. Also check out the helpful publications and Web sites on our Resources list (page 185), as well as the chapter Food for Thought & for Winter, which begins on page 180.

**Use a sharp knife or pruning shear to cut off pods when harvesting okra.** Harvest okra pods before they get to be 3 inches long; otherwise they become tough and stringy.

**Don't let cucumbers get blimplike and yellowish.** These chubby, jaundiced cucumbers are great if you're growing see Resources, page 185 for seed, but they're not great if you want plants to keep producing. Once cucumber fruits get old, plants stop producing and will not pick up the pace again even if mature cucumbers are removed.

**Pull up shallots** after the leafy tops have turned brown. We leave pulled plants on the ground for a few days and then place them on screens supported by sawhorses for 2 to 3 weeks to complete their drying. If rain threatens, they must be covered or moved indoors. Drying (or curing) toughens the outer skin and drives moisture from beneath the outer scales, which makes the bulbs last longer in storage. Afterward, cut away the tops, leaving about 1 inch of neck or stem attached to a bulb. Any bulbs with thick green necks should be used first.

**Harvest garlic** when a third to half of the leaves have turned yellow. If you wait until all the leaves have yellowed or browned, the cloves within the bulb begin to separate. Garlic bulbs with separated cloves do not store as well.

After harvesting garlic, allow the bulbs to dry in an airy location out of direct sunlight. This drying, or curing, process takes about 3 or 4 weeks and is necessary for prolonged storage of garlic.

*Pull up shallots when their leaves turn brown, and leave the shallots on the ground for a few days to begin curing.*

# Our Favorite Weeding Tools

**Ron:** This is not a good time to be a weed. We've launched our midseason assault on the green things that don't belong. Though we actually enjoy weeding, we don't mind using tools to make the task easier.

There are three types of hand weeders that I use most often. One is the Cape Cod weeder, a favorite of my wife and of many other gardeners. This dependable tool has been around for a long time and is available at most retail garden centers. The second weeder I use is one I received a few years ago for the purpose of testing and evaluating. It's called the CobraHead precision weeder because of the shape of the blade. It is fast becoming a favorite of mine. However, my current favorite is the hot bed weeder. I like the versatility of this tool and the fact that all the edges are sharp.

*Jen: My hands-down favorite tool is the Cape Cod weeder, which is great for ripping out stubborn grassy weeds. It's also very low maintenance: I simply wipe dirt from it and sharpen the blade edge once a year. I also find a rugged claw-type weeder useful for loosening tightly packed areas of overgrown weeds. For getting rid of newly germinated weed seedlings, my tool of choice is a sharpened hoe. It's easy on the back, and by slicing seedlings off at the soil surface, I'm not disturbing vegetable roots or exposing more weed seeds to the light they need for germination. (See Resources, page 185, for tool suppliers.)*

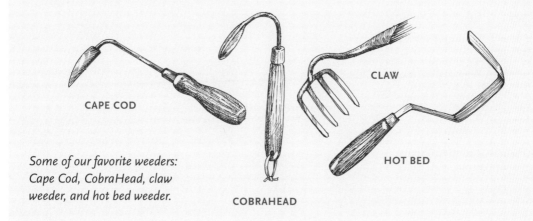

CAPE COD

CLAW

HOT BED

COBRAHEAD

*Some of our favorite weeders: Cape Cod, CobraHead, claw weeder, and hot bed weeder.*

# 11 **weeks after** average date of last frost

before last frost — ❄ — after last frost

11

↑
week of last frost

| | |
|---|---|
| **Long-season crops (sweet corn, tomato, pepper, eggplant, winter squash, pumpkin)** | → Side-dress plants with high-nitrogen natural fertilizer |
| **Cantaloupe, watermelon** | → Avoid overwatering as fruit nears maturity |
| | → Pinch off late-season blossoms |
| **Herbs** | → Cut back shabby-looking plants |
| **Buckwheat** | → Sow in vacant areas |
| **Kale** | → Sow seeds for late-season crop |
| **Parsley** | → Sow seeds in pots for indoor use |
| **Leaf lettuce, spinach, root crops** | → Make one last sowing |
| **Pea** | → Turn under vines after harvest is over |
| **Corn** | → Harvest just before cooking |
| **Summer squash, green bean** | → Keep harvesting regularly |
| **Escarole, endive** | → Tie outer leaves to blanch center leaves |

Dig a hole in a vacant spot in the garden and toss in kitchen wastes. This is just another way of composting. It will take from 2 to 3 weeks for most high-moisture materials such as lettuce leaves, apple peels, and orange rinds to decay. The smaller the materials, the quicker they'll break down.

## Seeding and Planting

**Sow seeds of buckwheat** in vacant areas of the garden. This so-called green-manure crop contributes organic matter to the soil when turned under, but what we like best about buckwheat is its ability to shade out weeds that would otherwise develop in these areas.

**Plant kale,** if you can find the seeds at garden centers or if you have some seed leftover from spring plantings. Kale planted now will be ready for harvest this fall. If hot weather persists, be prepared to shade seedlings until they are up several inches. Kale will also benefit from straw mulch placed around developing plants. Mmmmm! Our mouths are watering at the thought of sausage, kale, and white bean soup.

**Plant a few pots of parsley** for the windowsill herb garden. We used to dig up parsley plants in fall and then pot them for use in winter, but they didn't always transplant well because of damage to their taproot. So, now we just sow seeds directly into pots. Plant two or three seeds in a 6-inch pot. Try this with other culinary herbs, such as chives, chervil, and basil.

A supplementary light source may be needed to keep these herbs happy in winter.

**Make one more sowing** of leaf lettuce, spinach, and other leafy greens, as well as some root crops (radishes, kohlrabi, and carrots) to complete a late-season salad combination. It may seem late to plant carrots, but by using short-rooted varieties — such as Little Finger, Gold Nugget, Sweet & Short, and Tiny Sweet — and planting in raised beds or containers, it will be possible to get a crop by fall. The biggest problem may be to find a garden center that still has carrot and other vegetable seed at this time of year.

**Turn under old pea vines,** since they are a good source of nitrogen. Wait a few weeks to let plants break down in the soil, then plant a cover crop of winter rye. Winter rye will absorb some of the nitrogen released by the decayed pea plants. Next spring, when the winter rye is turned under, it will release nitrogen that will serve as a nutrient for newly planted vegetable crops. Ah, the marvels of nature!

## Maintenance

**Side-dress long-season crops** by applying a high-nitrogen natural fertilizer around each plant or along rows of plants in the vegetable garden. Compost and rotted manure are good alternatives to commercial natural fertilizers.

*Many potted herbs will thrive through the winter if grown near a sunny window and/or under a fluorescent-light fixture.*

## GREEN TOMATOES

IF TOMATO PLANTS are lush and fruit abounds but the bulk of the crop is languishing in a state of chronic green, one reason for this apparent malfunction might be cool summer weather. Usually at this time of year in our garden, we begin pinching off any new flower buds produced on tomato plants, since resultant fruits are unlikely to mature before first frost. Under the best growing conditions, it takes about 45 days for tomatoes to go from blossom to fully ripened fruit. In late summer, with days getting shorter and nights cooler, it takes even longer. Removing flowers now will enable tomato plants to direct more energy and food reserves to existing fruit and may help speed up ripening. Under no circumstances should you trim leaves from plants to promote ripening. That can result in sun scalding of fruit.

In any case, it might be a good idea to peruse cookbooks and place a tomato leaf or other bookmark on those pages with recipes that call for green tomatoes (see Resources, page 185, for a Web site with green tomato recipes).

The growth response of plants to compost or manure is slower than their response to water-soluble fertilizers, but these organic materials also have the benefit of improving the physical characteristics of soil.

**Be careful not to overwater cantaloupe and watermelon now.** Overwatering when melons are near maturity may reduce their sweetness and flavor. Also, pinch off blossoms that develop from this point on if you live in northern regions — they will not mature into ripe fruit before fall frost. Pulling off blossoms now will speed the ripening of remaining melons.

**Cut back herbs that look a bit shabby.** Some of the shabbiness may be the result of powdery mildew and other diseases, or

# WEED MANAGEMENT 101

It's a funny thing about weeds — sometimes it seems that the more you weed, the more weeds you get. Actually this is not a false perception arising from frustration at the futility of hours of effort to rid gardens of unwanted plants. In gardens where weeds once ruled, the soil has become a reservoir of weed seed; it is not unusual for gardens to have tens of thousands of weed seeds per cubic foot of soil. Yikes! When soil is disturbed, as it is when you pull up weeds and hoe or cultivate deeply, some weed seeds are briefly exposed to light. Seeing the light of day is all that these seeds need to begin germinating. Weed seeds can remain dormant in soil for many years even if the soil is moist and warm, conditions that seemingly should spur their germination. However, with many weed seeds, the controlling factor in their germination is light. If given even the briefest flash of light, weed seeds will begin to sprout.

So, to some extent, the more we weed and cultivate, the more weeds we get. Now, that sounds like an excuse to stop weeding. Don't! Get weeds out before they go to seed, slice off weeds at soil level with a hoe to lessen soil disturbance, and over time the number of weeds in the garden will diminish.

*Shearing shabby mint, oregano, and other bushy herbs will rejuvenate the plants and encourage new and healthy growth.*

insect damage. Leaf and stem diseases are common in years with frequent rains and high humidity. Cutting back the stems will encourage new and (hopefully) healthy growth.

**Tie heads of escarole and endive** or invert flower pots over plants to blanch (whiten) inner leaves. Blanching takes 2 to 3 weeks. Inner blanched leaves (the heart) have a mild flavor, whereas outer leaves are usually too bitter to use — discard them. You don't have to harvest blanched plants all at the same time; just cut the heads you need.

## Harvest

**Get it from "plot to pot — quick as a shot."** That's when sweet corn tastes best. If you can't pick sweet corn just before using it, then harvest ears early in the morning and store them in the refrigerator until needed.

**Pick summer squash and green beans** at least every other day, as they are maturing very rapidly now. Speaking of green beans, our favorite way to preserve the surplus is by pickling them. Maybe it's our technique (or lack thereof), but we find frozen green beans to be rubbery and canned ones to be mushy. Pickled ones always come out best for us. (Jen: My son is a huge fan of pickled green beans — pickled anything, really — and this is a great way to get him to eat his vegetables!)

*Blanch escarole and endive by tying the heads or by placing inverted flower pots over the plants.*

# 12–14 weeks after average date of last frost

## Dates in your area: _____ to _____

### SEED STARTING

- Carrot → Continue to sow in garden
- Winter rye → Sow as a cool-season cover crop
- Oats → Sow as a cool-season cover crop

### PLANTING

- Herbs → Start an indoor herb planting in a south- or west-facing window

### MAINTENANCE

- All crops
  → Continue to monitor for pests
  → At harvest, pull up and discard diseased and damaged plants
- Pumpkin, winter squash → Pinch off new blossoms
- Cauliflower → Blanch heads for 1 to 2 weeks before harvest
- Oregano, mint → Dig, divide, and replant
- Garlic, shallot → Select the best bulbs for replanting
- Dill, cilantro → Allow seeds on mature plants to fall to the ground and self-sow for next year
- Tomato → Do not cut off leaves to hasten fruit ripening
- Melon → Keep ripening fruit off the ground
- Strawberry
  → Apply high-nitrogen fertilizer to plants
  → Narrow existing rows to about 12 inches wide
- Corn → Chop up cornstalks after harvest

### HARVEST

- All crops
  → Freeze or can extra produce
  → Use soft or blemished produce immediately
- Tomato
  → Harvest and use split tomatoes right away
  → Can or freeze surplus tomatoes
- Zucchini → Continue to harvest
- Onion → Harvest when leafy tops have flopped over
- Bean, cucumber, corn, broccoli, cauliflower, summer squash, melon → Harvest as soon as they're ripe (fruit quality deteriorates after peak of ripeness)
- Tomato, pepper, eggplant → Harvest as needed (fruit quality will remain high if ripe fruit stays on plant for a few extra days)
- Green bean (bush and pole bean) → Leave overripe pods on plants and harvest as dry beans

YEAR_____

_____
_____
_____
_____
_____
_____
_____

YEAR_____

_____
_____
_____
_____
_____
_____
_____

YEAR_____

_____
_____
_____
_____
_____
_____
_____

# 12 **weeks after** average date of last frost

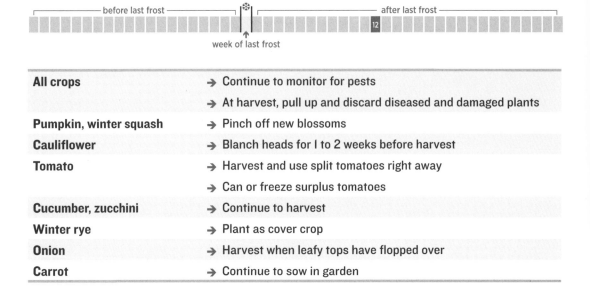

before last frost ——————————— ❄ ————————— after last frost ———————

↑
week of last frost

| All crops | → Continue to monitor for pests |
|---|---|
| | → At harvest, pull up and discard diseased and damaged plants |
| **Pumpkin, winter squash** | → Pinch off new blossoms |
| **Cauliflower** | → Blanch heads for I to 2 weeks before harvest |
| **Tomato** | → Harvest and use split tomatoes right away |
| | → Can or freeze surplus tomatoes |
| **Cucumber, zucchini** | → Continue to harvest |
| **Winter rye** | → Plant as cover crop |
| **Onion** | → Harvest when leafy tops have flopped over |
| **Carrot** | → Continue to sow in garden |

**B**uy some bales of straw. Use one or two in the fall to mulch garlic, shallots, and strawberry beds. Save the rest for use next gardening season. Straw can sometimes be hard to find, so buy a supply when it's available. (See Anticipation, page 144, for more information.)

## Seeding and Planting

**Pull up spent vegetable plants,** incorporate compost into the soil, and plant winter rye as a green-manure crop. This will keep garden soils healthy and productive if done routinely every year after crops are harvested.

**Continue to sow carrot seed.** Late-season seeding may not result in large carrots but that's not a problem since carrots can be eaten at almost any stage of development. We love the sweet, tasty baby carrots that late seeding gives us, especially if we dig the carrots after cool fall temperatures have settled in.

## Maintenance

**Continue to check for insect pests in the vegetable garden.** Cucumber beetles, cabbage worms, tomato hornworms, corn borers, and bean beetles are busy sampling the fruits of our labor. Select low-impact or "biorational" pesticides, as opposed to synthetic chemical pesticides,

*Pinching off new blossoms hastens the development of existing fruit on winter squash.*

when shopping for pest-control products.

**Pinch off new blossoms on pumpkins and other winter squash.** This will encourage faster development and larger size of existing fruit on pumpkin and squash vines.

**Protect the curd (head) of cauliflower** from exposure to sunlight so that it will develop the desirable white color. At 1 to 2 weeks before harvest, tie the leaves together above the curd. Failure to blanch results in bitter, not to mention ugly-looking, heads. Varieties sold as "self-blanching" aren't always reliably so. Speaking of ugly-looking heads (in our opinion), cauliflower now comes in colors reminiscent of 1960s tie-dyes. Typically, these varieties with green, purple, or orange heads don't need blanching. Some of these colored varieties of cauliflower are actually types of broccoli.

### Harvest

**Pull up and discard diseased and insect-damaged crops.** Otherwise these infected plants will perpetuate diseases and entice insects such as sap beetles to the garden.

**Harvest tomatoes that have split and use them immediately.** Split tomatoes left on plants will attract sap beetles and are also prone to invasion by decay-causing fungi. Splitting of tomatoes is most

*Blanch cauliflower by tying the leaves over the head.*

often caused by uneven watering. Certain varieties, like the very popular 'Sweet 100', are more prone to splitting than are others.

**Can or freeze the surplus tomato harvest.** To prepare tomatoes for freezing, drop them into a pot of

# SHEET COMPOSTING

IT'S A WISE and opportunistic gardener who can turn lemons into lemonade. It's an even wiser gardener who can turn lemon rinds into rich soil. An experienced gardener will immediately know that we are referring to the composting of organic wastes. At this time of the season, as more and more garden space becomes vacant with the harvesting of vegetable crops, we have an opportunity for turning good soil into great soil. This can be done by using a composting technique called sheet composting.

The first step is to dig a wide trench at least 1 foot deep in a vacant area of the garden. Spent plant materials from the garden and kitchen waste (vegetable matter only) are then placed into the trench and covered with soil. Between now and next spring, this plant debris will decay and contribute organic matter to the soil. The net result will be a rich, fertile soil and outstanding plant growth. This future yield, in turn, will enhance your reputation as a wise gardener, albeit one with an odd passion for lemons.

*Turn garden and kitchen wastes into rich soil right in the garden using the sheet-composting method.*

*Onions are ready to harvest when tops flop over and turn brown.*

boiling water for about 30 seconds. Then place tomatoes in a bowl of ice water to loosen the skins. Remove the skins, cut the tomatoes in half, squeeze out the seeds, and put the tomatoes into freezer bags. This is much easier than canning, but we prefer the taste of canned tomatoes over that of frozen ones.

**Harvest onions once their leafy tops have flopped over.** Pull up onions and lay them on top of the ground for a few days to dry. Then place bulbs with tops still attached in a dark, well-ventilated location for 2 to 3 weeks to cure. After curing, cut the tops to about 1 inch from the bulbs and store the bulbs in a cool, dry, airy place.

**Pick cucumbers early in the morning** while temperatures are still cool. Cucumbers have been referred to as nature's air conditioner. Perhaps it is their high water content, but whatever the reason, eating cucumbers on a hot day makes us feel . . . well, cool as a cucumber.

**Continue picking zucchini.** If you blink, they'll grow a couple of inches, so keep a close eye on the rapidly developing zucchini. However, if a zucchini has escaped attention, all is not lost. Detach the fruit and use it as a baseball bat or, better yet, in zapple pie (a recipe in *Serving Up the Harvest;* see Resources, page 185).

## ANTICIPATION

CARLY SIMON'S tune "Anticipation" could be the theme song for gardeners. We've learned by trial and error over the years that anticipating weather conditions, plant needs, and availability of supplies can make gardening more fruitful and less frustrating. A case in point: Do you grow garlic, shallots, or strawberries? If you do, you know that strawberry beds and fall-planted garlic and shallots require a protective covering of straw late in the year. Yet each fall, we're approached by friends who have been unable to locate a source of baled straw. Frustration!

The solution? Anticipate! The yearly harvest of straw is likely in now. Many garden and farm-supply dealers have ample quantities of this very useful mulching material, but supplies won't last. Buy now. We not only buy straw for fall mulching, but we also get enough for mulching the garden next spring.

# 13 weeks after average date of last frost

before last frost ——————— | ❄️ | ——————— after last frost ———————

↑
week of last frost

| | |
|---|---|
| **Tomato** | → Do not cut off leaves to hasten fruit ripening |
| **Melon** | → Keep ripening fruit off the ground |
| **Strawberry** | → Apply high-nitrogen fertilizer to plants |
| **Bean, cucumber, corn, broccoli, cauliflower, summer squash, melon** | → Harvest as soon as they're ripe (fruit quality deteriorates after peak of ripeness) |
| **Tomato, pepper, eggplant** | → Harvest as needed (fruit quality will remain high if ripe fruit stays on plant for a few extra days) |
| **Herbs** | → Start an indoor herb planting in a south- or west-facing window |

## Seeding and Planting

**Start an indoor herb garden** in a south- or west-facing window. Prepare pots of freshly seeded basil, parsley, cilantro, thyme, oregano, sage, and any other herb that will be used frequently in cooking through the winter months. Use a commercial potting soil to avoid weed and disease problems, but add about 1 teaspoon of limestone for each 6-inch pot. Many herbs prefer soils with a pH higher than that found in commercial potting mixes. Limestone will help to raise pH.

## Maintenance

**Do *not* cut off leaves on tomato plants to hasten fruit ripening.** Doing so will result in sun-scalded fruit. Tomato fruit with sun scald will have a large white or yellow blotch on the side of the fruit exposed to direct sunlight. Sun scald is also a problem with tomatoes that are staked, because the plants have fewer leaves than plants that are allowed to sprawl or grow in cages.

**Prevent ripening melons from rotting** by preventing contact with the wet ground. An easy way to do this is to place a flower pot, coffee can, or pile of straw beneath each melon.

**Give strawberry plants a light application of a high-nitrogen fertilizer now.** Fertilizer will help in the development of fruit buds for next year's crop. Apply 1 pound of actual nitrogen per

*Prevent fruit rot by placing a flower pot under a ripening melon.*

1,000 square feet. Actual nitrogen is calculated by multiplying the percent of nitrogen in the bag by the total weight of the package. For example, a 10-pound bag of fertilizer with 10 percent nitrogen contains 1 pound of actual nitrogen. You will need to apply the entire bag of fertilizer to get 1 pound of actual nitrogen over a 1,000-square-foot area.

## Harvest

**Find a harvest helper.** Arrange for someone — a neighbor, a relative, deer, or rabbits — to harvest your maturing vegetables if you're planning a vacation. Ask them to check on the crops every couple of days. Remember, harvesting ripe vegetables will keep plants productive.

# THE BASIL HARVEST

WE GENERALLY GET four or five major harvests of basil leaves during the growing season; we go into harvest mode whenever we see flower buds beginning to form at the ends of shoots. To ensure a good crop, each plant gets a dose of fertilizer as needed. Fertilizing and daily watering ensure that plants continue to grow with vigor.

In addition to plants we have in the garden, we also grow basil plants in 1-gallon nursery pots on the deck. When we grow them this way, less dirt splashes onto leaves during a rain or when we water the plants. A mulch of pea stones placed on the surface of the potting soil also helps keep basil leaves clean. An additional benefit of growing basil in pots is that we rarely have any problems with slugs eating the leaves.

What do we do with all this basil?

Most of it is converted into pesto. That's a lot of pesto, so we freeze the majority of it. We also dry some of the larger basil leaves and store them in airtight jars. Finally, we finely chop some, mix them with a small amount of water, and then place the mixture in ice cube trays for freezing. Once they're frozen, we pop out the cubes and store them in plastic freezer bags. We add the cubes as needed to sauces, soups, and other culinary creations.

Basil is just one of the crops that we're harvesting and processing now. Almost everything in our vegetable garden comes to maturity this month, and activity in our kitchen will be hotter than the weather.

# 14 weeks after average date of last frost

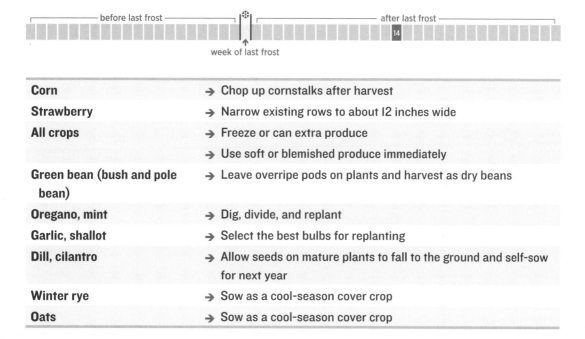

before last frost ——————————— | ✱ | ——————————— after last frost ———————————

↑
week of last frost

| | |
|---|---|
| **Corn** | → Chop up cornstalks after harvest |
| **Strawberry** | → Narrow existing rows to about 12 inches wide |
| **All crops** | → Freeze or can extra produce |
| | → Use soft or blemished produce immediately |
| **Green bean (bush and pole bean)** | → Leave overripe pods on plants and harvest as dry beans |
| **Oregano, mint** | → Dig, divide, and replant |
| **Garlic, shallot** | → Select the best bulbs for replanting |
| **Dill, cilantro** | → Allow seeds on mature plants to fall to the ground and self-sow for next year |
| **Winter rye** | → Sow as a cool-season cover crop |
| **Oats** | → Sow as a cool-season cover crop |

## Seeding and Planting

**Dig, divide, and replant herbs,** now that the weather is cooler and the soil is moist. Cool temperatures and moist soil mean plants will be less stressed than if you dug them on a hot, sunny, dry day. Herbs such as oregano and mint can easily get out of hand if not routinely reined in. The easiest way to keep these fast-spreading herbs manageable is to divide them every other year.

*Every two years, dig, divide, and quickly replant spreading herbs such as oregano and mint.*

**Sort through recently harvested shallots and garlic bulbs** and select bulbs to use as stock for replanting next month. The best planting stock is not necessarily the largest bulb, but one that has good shape — no distortions or abnormalities — and is clean and free of disease. While both shallots and garlic can be planted in fall, we've found little difference in growth and ultimate size between fall-planted and spring-planted shallots. So, we always plant garlic in the fall but usually leave shallots for the spring.

**Don't bother to pull up dill, caraway, fennel, and cilantro** (coriander) plants that have gone to seed. Let seed mature on the plants and then fall to the ground. Seeds will sprout next year, giving you a new crop of herbs without any expenditure of time, money, or effort. This process works best if plants for seed are given a permanent block of space in the vegetable or herb garden.

**Sow winter rye in vacant areas of the garden** at a rate of 2 to 3 pounds of seed per 1,000 square feet. After scattering seed over the soil, gently rake the areas to establish good seed-to-soil contact. It's not necessary to cover all the seed. The earlier cover crops are planted, the more they'll grow and the more organic matter there'll be for incorporating into the soil next spring. Winter rye is a good cover crop for northern gardens. It survives winter and will continue growing in spring. It must be turned under about 10 days prior to spring planting of crops.

**If you've been waiting all your life to sow your oats, now is the time to do it.** As an alternative to winter rye, seed the garden with oats at a rate of 2 pounds per 1,000 square feet. Unlike rye, oats will winter-kill and so will not regrow in spring.

## Maintenance

**Chop up cornstalks into small pieces** with a machete after the ears have been harvested. Chopping the stalks will speed their breakdown once you toss them onto the compost pile or turn them under in the garden—the smaller the pieces, the faster they'll break down. There's also some evidence that chopping cornstalks will destroy larvae of the European corn borer.

**Narrow strawberry rows to about 12 inches** by tilling between the rows or digging out stray plants. Strawberry plants are now forming the buds that will yield next spring's berries (these buds are not readily visible since they are deep inside the crowns of the plants), so be sure to water if soil gets dry at any point over the next 4 weeks.

*Narrow strawberry beds to about 12 inches by digging up or tilling plants that have strayed beyond the boundaries of the bed.*

**Begin garden cleanup.** At this time of year, leaves and stems of vegetables can look pretty shabby. Some of this is because the plants have reached the end of the line, but it may also be the result of disease and insect infestations. Cleaning up debris now will help reduce recurrence of the same problems next year. We usually bury diseased plants in a remote corner of the yard and toss the rest on the compost pile.

## Harvest

**Allow overmature green beans to fully ripen on the plants.** These can then be harvested as dry beans when pods turn brown. You can use these dry beans the same way you'd use any dry bean for baking, soups, and other bean dishes.

**Carefully inspect any vegetables that are to be stored** for any length of time, especially if diseases have been prevalent this year. Any vegetables that are not firm or that have blemishes should be used immediately or processed rather than stored. Any that are harvested green with the expectation they'll ripen in storage may turn into a rotten mess.

## RIPENING GREEN FRUIT

"OLD HABITS DIE HARD!" That's our comment on seeing the procession of green tomatoes lined up on people's sunny windowsills. This is not the best way to hasten ripening of tomato fruit. Tomatoes ripen best at temperatures close to 70°F (21°C). Temperatures near 90°F (32°C) might easily occur on a sunny windowsill, tomatoes will become soft before their red color has fully developed. By the time they turn red, they can be quite mushy (that's a technical term for very soft) and their quality will be greatly diminished.

So, what is the best way to ripen tomatoes indoors?

Well, if possible, let tomatoes ripen outdoors on the vine but pick them while they are still firm. But if for whatever reason ripening indoors is necessary, we recommend putting tomato fruit in a paper bag with a ripe apple and placing the bag where temperatures range between 60 and 75°F (15 and 24°C). Light is not necessary for ripening, though some light may increase the intensity of color.

Why the apple?

As fruit ripens, it gives off ethylene, a naturally occurring growth regulator. Ethylene, being a gas, can permeate the air and stimulate the ripening of adjacent fruit. This is the physiological basis for the old saying "One bad apple spoils the bunch." In the same way, ethylene given off by the apple will hasten ripening of tomatoes in the bag.

Another option for ripening mature green tomatoes (dull, light green in color) is to wrap each in a sheet of newspaper. Store the wrapped tomatoes at room temperature and check them every few days to see if they have ripened. Discard any that are rotting.

*To ripen green tomatoes, place them in a bag with a ripe apple.*

# 15–17 weeks after average date of last frost

## Dates in your area: _____ to _____

### SEED STARTING

- Herbs
  → Start seeds for growing indoors
- Radish
  → Sow seed for late crop
- Spinach
  → Sow seed for early harvest next year

### MAINTENANCE

- General
  → Test soil for limestone or sulfur deficiency, and apply if needed
- All crops
  → Pull weeds before they go to seed
- All nonhybrid crops
  → Save seeds for planting next year
- Tomato, eggplant
  → Pull up any plants not bearing fruit
  → Pinch off late-season blossoms
- Brussels sprouts
  → Pinch out tips to encourage sprout development
- Onion, shallot, garlic
  → Keep papery skins on bulbs when storing
- Tomato
  → Discard fruit with anthracnose symptoms

### HARVEST

- All crops
  → Can, freeze, or dry to preserve vegetables for winter use
  → Pull up and discard infected plant debris
- Potato
  → Harvest after tops have died down
- Cantaloupe
  → Harvest when stem and melon part easily
- Pepper
  → Leave some peppers on plants to turn red
- Plum tomato
  → Roast some of the harvest
- Pumpkin/winter squash
  → Harvest as soon as ripe
  → Cure for 1 to 2 weeks in a warm location

YEAR_____

YEAR_____

YEAR_____

# 15 **weeks after** average date of last frost

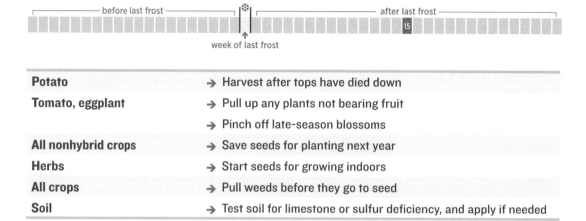

before last frost — ✳ — after last frost

15

↑
week of last frost

| Potato | → Harvest after tops have died down |
|---|---|
| Tomato, eggplant | → Pull up any plants not bearing fruit |
| | → Pinch off late-season blossoms |
| All nonhybrid crops | → Save seeds for planting next year |
| Herbs | → Start seeds for growing indoors |
| All crops | → Pull weeds before they go to seed |
| Soil | → Test soil for limestone or sulfur deficiency, and apply if needed |

Draw a plan of this year's vegetable garden before the memory fades. Knowing where this year's crops were planted allows us to rotate crops in next year's garden. Too often, we've convinced ourselves that we'd remember the planting scheme, but winter seems to numb our brains and render that memory useless.

## Seeding and Planting

**Start seeds of herbs** — including basil, parsley, cilantro, oregano, thyme, and chives — for growing indoors this winter. Herbs need lots of light for best growth, so place the plants near a window that receives direct sunlight most of the day or grow them under artificial light.

## Maintenance

**Continue to pull weeds** before they set seed and become a much larger nuisance next year, and the next, and the next . . . A plant like smooth pigweed can produce up to 100,000 seeds per plant, and ungerminated seeds can survive in the ground for up to 40 years. Yikes! If weeds in the garden already have seed heads, pull them in early morning. Seed heads are less likely to shatter at that time because of their high moisture content.

*Weeds such as pigweed are capable of producing thousands of seeds if not promptly removed from the garden.*

**Pinch off any new blossoms on tomatoes and eggplants.** If tomatoes have been slow to ripen this year, removing new flower buds now will divert a plant's energy to the development of existing fruit. So put inhibitions aside: Go out and pinch a tomato.

**Pull up tomato and eggplant plants** that are not bearing any fruit at this time, even if they have blossoms. It is too late in the season to expect any edible-size fruit from these crops, unless you live in a mild climate. In that case, allow the plants to continue growing. Experience will dictate your timing in future years.

**Have soil from vegetable gardens tested** to determine if you need to add limestone to raise pH or sulfur to lower pH. Since ground limestone and sulfur are slow to effect a change in soil pH, they are best applied in fall. Autumn rain and winter snow will carry limestone or sulfur into the soil. Look for soil-testing clinics offered by Master Gardener groups or contact your local Cooperative Extension office for the nearest soil-testing facilities (see Resources, page 185). Soil laboratories are usually less busy in the fall. (See Testing, Testing, page 16, for more details about how to collect soil samples.) Something as simple as soil pH can make a huge difference in the growth of plants. It's a good idea to have garden soils tested every 3 to 5 years to determine pH. The pH of garden soils can be influenced by a number of factors, such as precipitation, types of fertilizer used, and source of organic matter applied to soil.

## Harvest

**Wait until the tops of potato plants have died down before harvesting.** It is okay to dig under plants and pull out a few spuds for immediate use, but if potatoes are to be stored, they have

*Potatoes will keep longer in storage if harvested after the plants have died down.*

to be fully mature. Store potatoes for 1 week at room temperature to hasten the healing of any bruises. For long-term storage, keep potatoes in a cool but humid location.

**Experiment with saving seeds** from nonhybrid varieties of tomato, pepper, pea, and bean. Offspring from these plants will be the same from year to year. How to tell if your plants are nonhybrid? Check mail-order catalogs or seed packets for terms like *heirloom* and *open-pollinated.* Stay away from collecting seed from hybrids (created by combining different varieties). Offspring from hybrids can vary greatly in terms of vegetable yield, quality, and flavor. Air-dry seeds of pepper, pea, and bean, and store them in the refrigerator (see Saving Tomato Seeds, page 154). Store seeds with a packet of drying agent like powdered milk to help absorb any excess moisture. (See Resources, page 185, for more information on saving seeds.)

---

# THE "F" WORD

SINCE THERE MAY BE some sensitive readers out there, we should probably avoid using the "f" word. However, now that we are in the latter part of the growing season, the "f" word is often at the forefront of our minds.

Experience has taught us that once we get into early fall, a frost can occur at almost any time. Yes, frost! Children don't like to hear the word because it means the beginning of the end of their summer fun. Gardeners don't like to hear about it, since it means the end of the growing season for some of our favorite crops — namely, tomatoes, peppers, and beans.

We've long since given up trying to protect certain crops, such as tomatoes, from frost. Though covering plants keeps them alive, the quality of fruit deteriorates rapidly when plants are exposed to cold, if not freezing, temperatures. It's easy to forget that tomatoes are of tropical origin. Exposure to temperatures in the lower 40s and upper 30s (1 to 4°C) is enough to initiate deterioration of fruit. We'd rather pick the tomatoes and let near-ripe ones mature indoors or turn green fruit into relishes or pickled tomatoes.

# SAVING TOMATO SEEDS

WHEN SAVING SEEDS from nonhybrid tomatoes, such as heirloom varieties, pick tomatoes with the best-looking fruit from the healthiest, highest-yielding, and most vigorous plants. Remove seed-laden pulp from the tomato fruit and place it in a bowl of water. After about 24 hours, viable seeds will settle to the bottom of the bowl. Pour off separated pulp and water, rinse remaining seeds a few times in clean water, and place them on a paper towel to dry. Store dried seeds in glass jars or zip-lock bags in the refrigerator until the next growing season.

Squeeze seeds from a tomato or use a spoon to remove them.

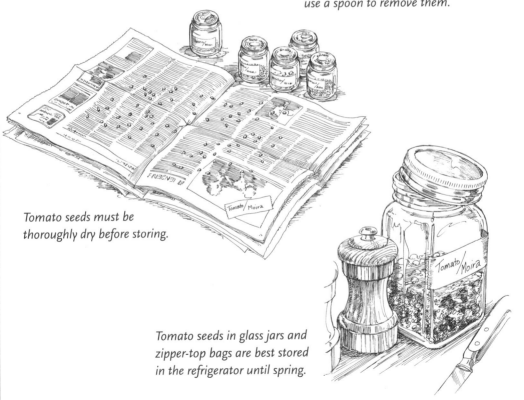

Tomato seeds must be thoroughly dry before storing.

Tomato seeds in glass jars and zipper-top bags are best stored in the refrigerator until spring.

# Troubleshooting in the Vegetable Garden

| SYMPTOM | DIAGNOSIS (AND CURE, IF POSSIBLE) |
|---|---|
| Failure of tomatoes, peppers, and eggplant to set fruit | • Most likely due to very warm or very cool nighttime temperatures |
| Blossom-end rot of tomatoes and peppers | • Varies with variety but is most often due to very dry soil conditions. Water well and mulch! |
| Poor plant growth with small fruit size on tomatoes | • The transplants were too old, too large, or overly hardened off. Young transplants of 6 weeks do best. |
| Cucumber plants wilt suddenly | • Bacterial wilt disease, most likely. Cucumber beetles carry the disease and introduce it as they feed on the plants. Control the beetles (see Maintenance, page 129). |
| Bitter-tasting cucumbers | • Caused by a substance called cucurbitacin, which develops in hot, dry weather. Keep plants watered during dry periods. |
| Poor fruit set on cucumbers and squash | • Usually due to poor pollination. Get yourself a bee or two (or 2,000) or an artist's paintbrush to transfer pollen to female flowers. |
| Forked or misshapen carrots | • Stones or large clods in the soil will cause roots to branch or take on an abnormal shape. Carrots crowded in the row will sometimes twist about one another. |
| Poor sprout development on Brussels sprouts | • This happens when temperatures are too high. Plant Brussels sprouts only for late-fall harvest. Pinch stem tips when first side buds are forming. |
| Poor root development of radishes | • High temperatures and long days stimulate shoot and seed stalk development at the expense of root development. Plant radishes early or late in the season, but don't grow them in summer unless you live in Alaska. |

# 16 weeks after average date of last frost

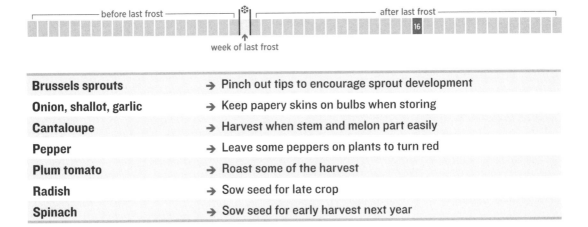

| Brussels sprouts | → Pinch out tips to encourage sprout development |
| Onion, shallot, garlic | → Keep papery skins on bulbs when storing |
| Cantaloupe | → Harvest when stem and melon part easily |
| Pepper | → Leave some peppers on plants to turn red |
| Plum tomato | → Roast some of the harvest |
| Radish | → Sow seed for late crop |
| Spinach | → Sow seed for early harvest next year |

Start a compost pile if you don't already have one. Incorporating compost into garden soil is the best way to sustain fertile soil and enhance the growth of plants. Compost supplies essential plant nutrients, prevents soil compaction, improves the nutrient- and water-holding ability of soil, and aids in warding off root-rot diseases. There's no need to build extravagant bins or to buy expensive compost barrels. Just pile up leaves and organic debris in an out-of-the-way corner of the backyard — or front yard if you have a penchant for organic exhibitionism. The rate of decomposition of organic matter can be hastened by turning the pile once a month. Don't bother to buy "compost activators" that claim to speed composting. In studies at the University of Massachusetts, commercial activators were found to have no effect on the rate of composting.

## Seeding and Planting

**Sow seed of radish.** Most varieties mature in about 28 days, though it may take a little longer at this time of year. Light frosts will not harm radish and may even enhance its flavor.

**Sow seeds of spinach.** Spinach seeded now can be kept in the ground over winter if covered with a floating row cover. The spinach can be harvested in very early spring.

## Maintenance

**Pinch out tips of Brussels sprouts.** In response, plants will redirect their energy to development of sprouts. Some gardeners like to remove leaves below developing sprouts, but this is not necessary to encourage maturation of sprouts. Sprouts taste best after plants have been exposed to some very cool temperatures.

## Harvest

**Be careful not to remove outer skins of onions, shallots, and garlic** when storing these vegetables for winter. The papery skins protect the bulbs from dehydration.

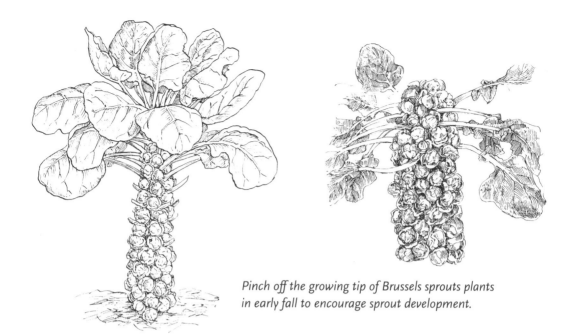

*Pinch off the growing tip of Brussels sprouts plants in early fall to encourage sprout development.*

**Gently push on the stem attaching a cantaloupe to its vine.** If the stem comes loose easily, the cantaloupe is ripe. If there is resistance, let it be. Also, use your nose to test the ripeness of cantaloupe. Sniff the stem end of fruit. If it smells sweet, it is ready to pick. The nose knows.

**Leave some peppers on plants** and allow these to turn red before harvesting. Red peppers have a milder, sweeter taste than green peppers do. Of course, when frost threatens, all bets are off; pick them all, regardless of color or size.

**Try roasting some plum tomatoes to concentrate their flavor.** Slice tomatoes in half lengthwise, place them on a baking sheet, drizzle them with olive oil and sprinkle with sea salt, and roast them in a 250°F (120°C) oven for 3 hours, or until tomatoes are soft but not juicy. Freeze roasted plum tomatoes you don't plan to use within a few days.

*A ripe cantaloupe will slip free from its vine when gentle thumb pressure is applied to the stem at the point of attachment.*

# 17 weeks after average date of last frost

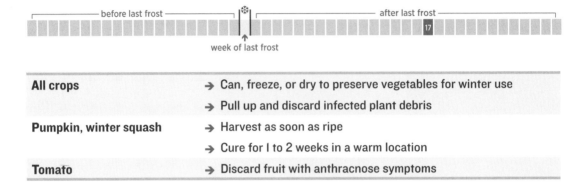

| All crops | → Can, freeze, or dry to preserve vegetables for winter use |
| | → Pull up and discard infected plant debris |
| Pumpkin, winter squash | → Harvest as soon as ripe |
| | → Cure for I to 2 weeks in a warm location |
| Tomato | → Discard fruit with anthracnose symptoms |

## Maintenance

**Spend some quality time with your garden spade.** Turn over garden soil before the ground freezes. As British actor Richard Briers once said, "An hour's hard digging is a good way of getting one's mind back in the right perspective."

Also start the garden-debris cleanup in earnest. During wet summers especially, many garden plants have been ravaged by various leaf diseases. There's no sense in waiting to rid the garden of infected plants or plant parts. Diseased vegetables should be pulled up and discarded or buried. Try to leave behind as little of the infected plant debris as possible.

## Harvest

**Harvest pumpkins as soon as they are ready** — that is, when the rind is hard and the color is uniformly deep orange. Even Peter Peter Pumpkin Eater knew that pumpkins must be picked when ripe, lest they be invaded by varmints or disease. Pumpkins that are to be stored shouldn't be exposed to freezing temperatures. Frost on the pumpkin may make a great calendar picture, but it makes mush out of the pumpkin. Frosted squash and pumpkins will be okay if used immediately, but they will not keep very long when placed in storage. Also, for longer storage life, leave 2-inch handles (stems) attached to the fruit.

**Place pumpkins and winter squash in a warm spot** for 1 or 2 weeks to enable skins or rinds to fully cure. They'll keep much better. Then store these crops in a cool (but not cold) location that is dry and dark. Unlike apples, potatoes, turnips, rutabagas, and onions (which all prefer storage temperatures near 45°F [7°C]), winter squash and pumpkins keep best at storage temperatures between 55 and 65°F (13 and 18°C). Pumpkins stored at a temperature of about 55°F (13°C) with moderate humidity will keep for 2 to 3 months. In earlier times, folks found the bedroom provided ideal storage conditions and often stashed winter squash and pumpkins beneath their beds. A few episodes of memory failure followed by less than subtle accusations regarding personal hygiene eventually led to other storage arrangements.

**Discard tomatoes with small sunken or dimpled areas** that may be red, orange, or black. The dimples are a symptom of anthracnose, a disease that quickly leads to rotting of the fruit.

# DEER IN THE GARDEN

W E RECENTLY ENTERED our garden to find that we were hosts to a meeting of the Berkshire Deer Assembly (BDA). The theme of the meeting was "Delectable Edibles." Participants were actively involved in a workshop on fall vegetable consumption when we crashed the assembly. As nonmembers of the organization, our presence caused offense, and the deer hastily adjourned to the woods.

Deer are particularly troublesome any time there is tasty and succulent new growth in the garden. Our primary defense against their dining preferences has been the use of repellents.

Check local garden centers for deer repellents that are biodegradable and safe to use in vegetable gardens. These often contain natural products such as blood meal, garlic oil, hot pepper, coyote urine, and putrid egg base.

The key to using repellents is to alternate products so that deer do not become used to any one material. Repellents also have to be reapplied frequently, especially after a rain. Over the years, we have found the most effective repellent to be the family dog. Until the dog moved on to the kennel in the sky, there were few meetings of the BDA at our garden.

Another way to get a leg up on the deer problem is with the use of animal urine. Coyote, wolf, and bobcat varieties are all available in the garden marketplace, and field tests in Alaska indicate that the products actually work quite well. Our question is, how do they collect the stuff?

*A high fence is the best defense against deer invasions into your vegetable garden. Deer can easily jump over a 6-foot-high fence.*

# 18–21 weeks after average date of last frost

## Dates in your area: _____ to _____

### PLANTING

| | |
|---|---|
| • Chive | → Dig and pot up a clump for indoor use |
| • Garlic | → Plant now |

### MAINTENANCE

| | |
|---|---|
| • General | → Save wood ashes to incorporate into garden soil |
| • All crops | → Empty and clean window boxes, patio boxes, and other containers |
| | → Turn under crop remnants |
| • Tomato | → Pull up and clean support stakes and cages |
| | → Inspect stored tomatoes |
| • Cabbage, broccoli, cauliflower | → Leave spent plants in the garden to deter cabbage worms in next year's crop |
| • Buckwheat | → Turn under after frost kills plants |
| • Garlic | → Prepare soil for planting |
| • Rhubarb | → Spread well-rotted manure over bed |

### HARVEST

| | |
|---|---|
| • Ornamental gourd | → Harvest when ripe |
| | → Wash and cure for several weeks in a warm, airy location |
| • Root crops (turnip, rutabaga, beet, carrot), kale, chard | → Harvest as needed and leave the rest in the garden to sweeten in cold weather |
| • Shell (dry) bean | → Harvest when plants and pods are brown |
| • Brussels sprouts | → Harvest sprouts after frost |
| • Pumpkin, squash | → Clean and toast seeds for snacks |
| • Popcorn/ornamental corn | → Harvest and dry |

YEAR_____

YEAR_____

YEAR_____

# 18 weeks after average date of last frost

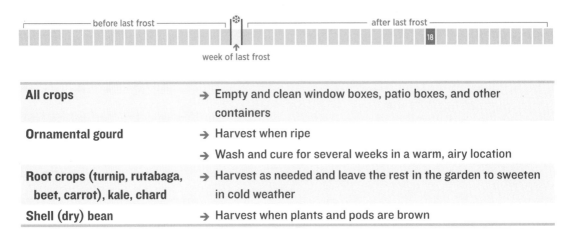

before last frost

week of last frost

after last frost

18

| All crops | → Empty and clean window boxes, patio boxes, and other containers |
|---|---|
| Ornamental gourd | → Harvest when ripe |
| | → Wash and cure for several weeks in a warm, airy location |
| Root crops (turnip, rutabaga, beet, carrot), kale, chard | → Harvest as needed and leave the rest in the garden to sweeten in cold weather |
| Shell (dry) bean | → Harvest when plants and pods are brown |

Make note of areas where wilt diseases infected vegetable crops. Many fungi that cause wilt diseases live in the soil. Plan to grow unrelated crops in those areas next year. Soilborne diseases may indicate areas that drain poorly. If so, it may be better to abandon such areas or make raised beds there for growing crops.

## Maintenance

Empty window boxes, patio pots, and other containers that held annual herbs. Brush soil from the surfaces of containers and wash them with a solution of 1 part household bleach to 9 parts water. Wooden containers should be treated with a wood preservative such as linseed oil.

## Harvest

**Allow ornamental gourds to reach full maturity** before harvesting. A gourd is mature when the stem is brown and dry and when the rind is hard. Wash harvested gourds in warm, soapy water and rinse them in clear water. Cure cleaned-up gourds by spreading them out on several layers of newspaper in a warm, airy spot for several weeks. Turn gourds every few days for uniform curing. Large gourds generally keep longer than small ones, which usually last 4 to 6 months.

**Harvest root crops** — turnips, rutabagas, beets, carrots, and others — as needed, but leave the rest to continue their growth. The same is true for leafy greens like kale and chard. Frost will not hurt them and can actually improve their flavor.

*Gourds were at one time used as food and household utensils. Today, they are used primarily in decorative displays.*

**Harvest shell (dry) beans** when plants and pods are completely brown. Pull up the entire plants, tie them in bunches, and hang the bunches to dry until the pods are brittle. To shell the beans (that is, remove the pods), place the pods in a burlap bag or old bedsheet and beat them with a thin, flat board or broom to separate beans from pods. Wait for a breezy day or use an electric fan to separate beans from chaff (pod fragments), or dump the beans on a tarp or bedsheet and toss them in the air, letting the breeze blow away the chaff. You'll want a partner for this project.

*When pods of shell beans are fully dried, put them in a burlap bag and beat with a stick to free beans from their pods.*

*Seperate the beans from the chaff by pouring them onto a tarp and tossing them in the air, allowing the wind to blow away the chaff.*

# KALE

A FAVORITE GARNISH for dishes served in restaurants now and through the winter is a little bundle of curly leaf kale. A garnish is often perceived as something that makes a dish look pretty and the food perhaps a little more interesting (though it doesn't do much for a hot dog) but is not something you'd want to eat. That's too bad, because kale is great tasting and one of the most nutritious vegetables. We like to use it in soups, or sautéed with olive oil and Canadian bacon, or cooked with sausage.

Kale, a cabbage relative, is a cool-weather crop. Its flavor is enhanced by exposure to cool, even frosty weather. Unfortunately, unless you planted some this summer, you'll have to get your kale at the produce market. Or will you?

A popular fall ornamental plant still available at many garden centers is flowering kale, sometimes referred to as flowering

*Kale can be left to overwinter in the garden in most areas of the country except for the northernmost states.*

cabbage. The reddish, purple, and white leaves add a splash of bright color to the fading landscape. The plant is so showy that most people forget that it is an edible vegetable. Individual leaves may be picked from the plants as needed in the kitchen. This is one situation where you can have your cake . . . uh, *kale* . . . and eat it, too.

# 19 weeks after average date of last frost

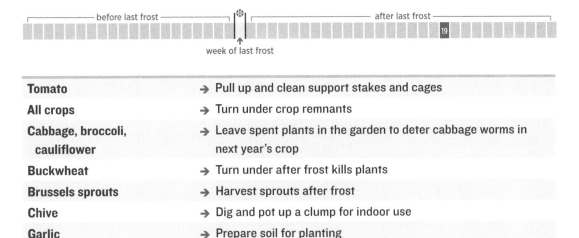

before last frost — | — after last frost —

week of last frost

| Tomato | → Pull up and clean support stakes and cages |
| All crops | → Turn under crop remnants |
| Cabbage, broccoli, cauliflower | → Leave spent plants in the garden to deter cabbage worms in next year's crop |
| Buckwheat | → Turn under after frost kills plants |
| Brussels sprouts | → Harvest sprouts after frost |
| Chive | → Dig and pot up a clump for indoor use |
| Garlic | → Prepare soil for planting |

## Seeding and Planting

**Pot up a clump of chives.** Water soil well around a clump of chives and then dig it up. Divide the clump into several smaller clumps. Pot up a couple of these for growing indoors, cut back the tops, and leave the pots outside for two or three hard frosts before bringing them into the

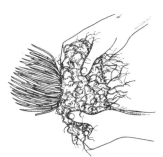

*Divide a large clump of chives into smaller clumps of 3 to 5 bulblets for potting up.*

house. Replant the unpotted clumps back into the garden. The leaves will probably flop but don't worry about it. After a couple of weeks, when the roots are reestablished, cut back the floppy leaves. New shoots will come up.

**Prepare garden soil for planting garlic.** Incorporate some well-rotted manure or compost into the soil. We also like to work in some wood ash; the potassium found in it promotes healthy growth of garlic.

## Maintenance

**Begin pulling up tomato stakes** when plants are no longer productive. After pulling up the stakes, brush off the soil. Spores of the fungus that causes early blight

can persist on stakes through winter, so apply a copper-based fungicide such as liquid copper, lime sulfur, or Bordeaux mix (copper sulfate and lime) to the stakes to destroy the blight-causing fungus. When the stakes are dry, apply a wood preservative such as linseed oil. Follow the same procedure for bean trellises and other wooden plant-support structures.

**Turn under remnants of vegetable crops** to a depth of 6 inches or so. Vegetation will decompose and contribute organic matter to the soil. Most disease-causing organisms that infected any crops this year will die when worked into the soil. Turning over soil in late fall, either with a tiller or by hand with a garden spade, can help control insects such as corn borer, corn earworm, cucumber beetle, squash bug, and vine borer because it exposes them to harsh weather conditions. Fall tillage also makes spring soil preparation easier.

**Leave spent plants of cabbage, broccoli, and cauliflower** in the garden through winter. Research has shown that a parasite of the imported cabbage worm (a key pest of cabbage family plants) spends the winter in the cocoon stage on the old plants. In spring, the parasite moves onto the newly planted cabbage crop and is there to attack the cabbage worm when it arrives. We usually pull up old cabbage plants, but in the future we plan to leave them in place to see if the parasite will reduce problems with cabbage worms on the following year's crop.

**Turn under buckwheat** after frost has killed the plants. Or, leave it until spring. It decomposes rapidly.

## Harvest

**Harvest Brussels sprouts** after Jack Frost has mellowed them. Cut or break off sprouts as needed, but don't harvest all of them unless you have an insatiable craving for the vegetable. Remaining sprouts will continue to grow well into the fall.

# Rhubarb Out of Season

**Ron:** As a little sprout many years ago, I remember my mother serving stewed rhubarb for dessert during winter months. The rhubarb came from the supply she had canned the previous spring. It was a treat to have the tart rhubarb at that time of year.

**Jen:** *Though we don't put up canned rhubarb like Grandma did, my mother and I do freeze rhubarb. We simply cut the washed stems into 1-inch pieces and put them in freezer bags.*

*Those gardeners who didn't have the forethought to can or freeze rhubarb last spring can still enjoy some this winter by forcing roots of rhubarb into producing edible pink stalks indoors.*

*To do this, dig up some roots now and place them, with soil, into large plastic pots or wooden boxes. Leave the pots outdoors under a tarp or put them in an unheated garage or shed where the roots will be exposed to freezing temperatures. When ready to force some rhubarb, bring the pots into a dark corner of the basement. After the soil thaws, water as needed to keep the soil moist. Within a few weeks, there'll be shoots of rhubarb to turn into a warm and tasty winter treat. Remember to use the leaf stalks only, not the leaves themselves. The leaves contain chemicals that are poisonous to humans and animals.*

# 20–21 weeks after average date of last frost

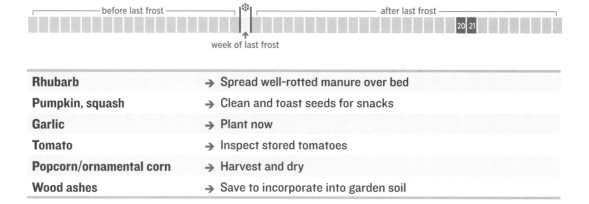

before last frost ─────────────────────── | ❄ | ───────────────── after last frost ─────────────────

↑
week of last frost

| Rhubarb | → Spread well-rotted manure over bed |
|---|---|
| Pumpkin, squash | → Clean and toast seeds for snacks |
| Garlic | → Plant now |
| Tomato | → Inspect stored tomatoes |
| Popcorn/ornamental corn | → Harvest and dry |
| Wood ashes | → Save to incorporate into garden soil |

Save the ashes if you burn wood in the fireplace or woodstove. Wood ash is high in potassium (2.8 to 8.6 percent), a nutrient that is especially useful to root crops such as carrots, turnips, radishes, and onions. Be aware that wood ash is also high in calcium (14 to 28 percent), so do not use it if soil is already alkaline (has a high pH). If you plan to use wood ash as a soil amendment in the garden, store it in a dry location until it is needed. Scatter the ash over the vegetable garden at no more than 2½ pounds per 100 square feet if soils are known to be acidic. Other plant nutrients present in wood ash are phosphorus (0.8 to 3 percent), magnesium (0.8 to 2.8 percent), and sulfur (0.3 to 0.5 percent).

Fill a garbage can with garden soil and place it in a location where it will not freeze. We use this soil to cover kitchen wastes that are tossed onto the compost pile through winter. Covering the organic waste with soil will keep rodents and other animals from getting at it.

## Seeding and Planting

**Plant garlic now.** Some studies have shown that eating garlic regularly helps lower cholesterol levels and blood pressure. Garlic is also high in selenium, a mineral that has cancer-fighting properties. Maybe we need to change that old saying "An apple a day keeps the doctor away" to "A garlic bulb a day will keep the grim reaper away." Garlic can be planted any time in mid-fall.

## Maintenance

**Spread a 1-inch-deep layer of fresh horse manure** over areas of the vegetable garden where a winter cover crop has not been planted. This amount of horse manure will provide enough nitrogen and potassium to sustain growth of vegetable crops next season. If you can't find a fresh horse, apply aged horse manure. If you can't find an aged horse, apply compost. Turn over the soil with a spading fork or tiller to incorporate the organic matter. Annual applications of organic matter will help sustain good soil structure and fertility.

**Mound soil into raised beds** in the area of the garden where early crops are to be sown next spring. Soil in raised beds will drain quickly after the ground thaws. It will also warm quickly, allowing for an early start to root crops, peas, and leafy greens.

**Apply a layer of well-rotted manure over rhubarb beds.** Never use fresh manure around these plants because it promotes certain diseases of rhubarb.

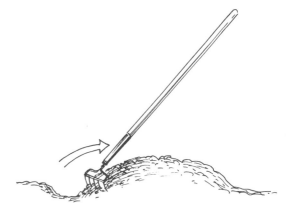

*Rake garden soil into mounds that are 6 to 8 inches high and 12 to 24 inches wide. These mounds or raised beds will allow for early planting of cool-season crops next spring.*

**HE SAYS**

# Putting More Pop into Your Popcorn

**Ron:** As a youngster, one of my fun tasks on Sunday evenings was to go into the corn crib at my grandparents' farm and shell some popcorn to take home. Then, with a big bowl of freshly popped popcorn, I would sit back with my parents and siblings and watch the adventures of Hopalong Cassidy. (*Jennifer: Ugh! Not another old cowboy reference!*)

Popcorn is not a crop grown by many home gardeners today. One reason may be the amount of space required to grow a corn crop. I suspect another reason may be past failures to get good popping out of homegrown popcorn.

Poor popping is most likely due to improper drying of the corn. Popcorn must be left on the cornstalk until the stalk turns brown. The corn husks must dry completely and the corn kernels must become hard. Once harvested, the ears should be husked and then stored in a mesh bag or an open-weave basket (like a peach basket) for curing.

To cure popcorn, place the ears in a warm, dry, and well-ventilated place, such as an attic or garage, for 3 weeks. Afterward, shell the corn by rubbing one ear against another to release the kernels. Seal the kernels in airtight glass jars and store them in a cool location.

On the first crispy fall evening, pop up a batch of the corn, plop down in the recliner, and turn on the gardening channel, since Hopalong is long gone.

## Harvest

**Harvest popcorn and ornamental Indian corn** after the stalks have thoroughly dried. Further drying of the ears in an airy location is essential to prevent mold from developing during storage. This precaution also holds true for drying shell beans for winter use.

**Inspect the green tomatoes** that you wrapped in newsprint and stored for fall use. The ones that would turn red will have done so by now. The ones that are still green will probably remain green, so it would be best to use them as green tomatoes in relishes, or just fry them.

**Don't throw away the seeds when dismantling pumpkins** for cooking or for jack-o'-lanterns. The seeds make a nutritious snack food when roasted. Clean the seeds; toss them in a little vegetable oil and salt; spread seeds onto a cookie sheet; and roast them at low heat for about 30 minutes or so, stirring now and then to keep them from burning. Hull-less varieties (their seeds lack a seed coat) like 'Godiva', 'Kakai', and 'Snackjack' have been developed specifically for seed roasting, but we like the crunch of seeds with hulls. Interestingly, early growers favored edible seeds over the pumpkin flesh.

*Save seeds from pumpkins for roasting. Pumpkin seeds are very nutritious; they're high in manganese, magnesium, phosphoros, protein, and vitamin K.*

# Garden Smells

**Ron:** "This smell reminds me of the old days on the farm when we were harvesting onions," I said to Jennifer as we pulled up our crop of shallots earlier this week.

While some may not find the smell of onions or shallots particularly pleasant, it's not the scent that's important to me, it's the vision that it evokes. *Eau de onion* is just one of the aromas in the air that seem to say "Harvesttime!" There is also the scent of maturing cornstalks and of pungent tomato foliage, and the sweet aroma of ripening melons. These are the fragrances that conjure up visions of cornucopias of fruits and vegetables.

*Jen: The smells at harvesttime are certainly poignant (what usually gets me nostalgic is the smell of ripening tomatoes and bruised leaves as I brush past), but it is the way soil smells in springtime that really gets me charged up about gardening. I'm sure you know what I'm talking about — that earthy, fresh scent. Did you know that the distinctive spring smell of the soil is actually caused by beneficial bacteria, actinomycetes, which help break down dead plants into humus?*

# PLANTING GARLIC

GARLIC is native to the Mediterranean region, and ancient Romans grew it for food and medicinal uses. Though the nobility refused to eat garlic, since the flavor was too strong for their delicate palates, they did feed it to roosters to bolster their prowess in cockfights, to laborers to make them stronger, and to soldiers to give them courage. Maybe it was the strong smell of a Roman soldier's breath as opposed to his courage that chased away the enemy.

Today, garlic knows no social bounds. Gentry and common folk share a love for the pungent bulb. We witness the popularity of garlic every year when we travel to the annual Garlic Festival in nearby Saugerties, New York. The enormity of the event and the size of the crowd are most impressive. Our primary reason for going is to get some new varieties of garlic to add to the 30 (!) that we already grow in our garden. "Garlic is garlic" some might say. That really isn't the case, as we discovered in sampling the many varieties being sold by the dozens of vendors at the festival. For example, the flavor of 'Spanish Roja' is so spicy that it's almost like eating a hot pepper. Near the other end of the spectrum is the popular 'German White' variety, with a much milder flavor.

Almost all the varieties we grow are of the hardneck type, as opposed to the softneck type. We've found that hardneck varieties are better suited to our climate and produce six to eight large cloves per bulb. 'Polish Jen' and 'Music' are the varieties we like best, because of their spicy flavor, large cloves, and longevity in storage. Softneck types produce bulbs with more, but smaller, cloves and are better suited to a warmer climate.

Garlic is an easy crop to grow but does best in deep, nutrient-rich soil, well amended with organic matter. Each year, we spread approximately 1 inch of screened compost over the soil. Next, we scatter a general-purpose natural fertilizer according to label recommendations. We're ready to plant our garlic as soon as we've turned over the soil.

At planting, we separate individual cloves from the bulbs and set them into the ground, pointed-side up, at a depth of 2 inches. The largest cloves produce the largest bulbs. We space the cloves 4 inches apart within the rows, and we save space by planting double rows 6 inches apart. Once the ground begins to freeze, we cover rows with a thick layer of straw. In spring, at the first appearance of garlic shoots, we uncover plants but leave the straw alongside the plants as a mulch.

*Don't separate individual garlic cloves from the bulbs until the day of planting.*

*In cold regions, cover garlic plantings with 3 inches of straw. When new growth appears in spring, remove the mulch from the plants but leave it between the rows.*

# 22–29 weeks after average date of last frost

### Dates in your area: _____ to _____

## SEED STARTING

| | |
|---|---|
| ▪ Garden cress | → Sow seed indoors |
| ▪ Herbs | → Start seed for indoor growing |
| ▪ Garlic | → Plant now, if you haven't already |

## MAINTENANCE

| | |
|---|---|
| ▪ General | → Shred leaves before composting |
| ▪ All crops | → Begin planning for next year |
| | → Clean pots and flats for seed starting |
| | → Use dishwashing soap and water to clean insects from indoor edibles |
| ▪ Asparagus | → Cut down shoots after a killing frost |
| | → Apply limestone and compost to bed |
| ▪ Herbs | → Put leggy indoor plants under lights |
| | → Check indoor plants for insect pests |
| ▪ Parsnip | → Cover plants with soil if leaving them in the ground until spring or straw if harvesting during winter |
| ▪ Garlic, shallot, strawberry | → Place mulch over beds when ground begins to freeze |
| ▪ Leek | → Cover with a layer of straw if keeping plants in garden |
| ▪ Rosemary | → Keep potting soil moist for healthy plants indoors |

## HARVEST

| | |
|---|---|
| ▪ Root crops | → Do not wash before storing |
| | → Store in a trash can sunk in the ground and covered with straw |
| ▪ Beet | → Leave 1 inch of stem attached to harvested beet roots |
| ▪ Carrot | → Trim leafy tops to 1 inch above the root before storing carrots |
| ▪ Pumpkin | → Pumpkins from fall decorations can be used in cooking, unless they were carved |

YEAR_____

YEAR_____

YEAR_____

# 22–23 weeks after average date of last frost

before last frost | week of last frost | after last frost
22 23

| Asparagus | → Cut down shoots after a killing frost |
| | → Apply limestone and compost to bed |
| Herbs | → Put leggy plants indoors under lights |
| Garden cress | → Sow seed indoors |
| Root crops | → Do not wash before storing |
| | → Store in a trash can sunk in the ground and covered with straw |
| Leaves | → Shred before composting |

Store some shredded leaves in large garbage bags. Shredded leaves will break down faster than whole leaves. Shredded leaves will not only make neat beanbag-type chairs for the living room, but will also provide a supply of mulch for next season's vegetable garden.

Create a separate compost pile just for tree leaves. When decomposed, leaves form a rich compost product that is relatively clean of weed seeds. Because it is "clean," we like to use leaf compost as a primary component of potting soil for vegetable seedlings. We usually shred the leaves with a lawn mower before tossing them onto the compost pile with some grass clippings. The latter is a good source of nitrogen to hasten the composting process.

### Seeding and Planting

Plant a few pots of garden cress, a fast-growing vegetable that resembles parsley but tastes like watercress. Sow seeds on the surface of soil, since they require light for germination. Place pots in a sunny but cool window — an east-facing window works well. It takes only about 2 weeks to go from seed to harvesting cress. Cut some shoots as needed for use in salads and sandwiches.

*Keep a pot or two or garden cress on the windowsill through winter. The tangy flavor of garden cress will add some zest to salads and sandwiches.*

*Asparagus shoots will continue to photosynthesize until killed by frost. Though some growers leave the fernlike shoots in the garden through winter, we prefer to cut down and discard the shoots as a means of controlling pests and diseases of asparagus.*

## Maintenance

**Cut down the fernlike shoots of asparagus** once you've had a killing frost. Remove the shoots from the garden, since they may harbor asparagus beetles and/or the fungus that causes rust disease. Since asparagus grows poorly in acidic soil, you may need to apply ground limestone to the soil (but only after having the soil tested to determine the amount of limestone needed). After working in the limestone, spread a 1- to 2-inch layer of compost or rotted manure over the asparagus bed.

**Apply limestone and other slow-to-dissolve soil amendments** such as rock phosphate and greensand (a natural potassium source) to garden soils this fall if needed, as indicated by your soil test results. Work these materials into the soil to a depth of about 8 inches. All of these amendments are slow to release their mineral nutrients, so fall is the best time to apply them. They'll have the winter months to dissolve.

**Drain outdoor faucets and rain barrels.** Drain and bring in garden hoses as well.

**Wash spraying equipment** with a solution of 1 cup ammonia in 1 gallon of water. Rinse with clean water and hang the sprayer to air-dry. Be sure to clean the screen, nozzle, and hose as well.

**Review the owner's manual for your tiller** if you're not familiar with the pre-winter maintenance the tiller may require. Change the oil, drain fuel, or add a fuel stabilizer to the gas tank, scrub soil from tines, and remove grit from around engine parts.

**Place potted herbs under a fluorescent light** if they are getting leggy. Usually, natural light from a window during the fall and winter is not enough to keep these sun-loving plants happy. We know how they feel.

## Harvest

**Examine root crops and all storage crops carefully** and store only those in perfect condition. Don't wash crops before storing. The skins of vegetables offer natural protection against disease infection, and you don't want to cause any abrasions or disruptions in this natural barrier to disease.

**Sink a trash can into the ground** to create a mini–root cellar for winter storage of carrots, beets, and other hardy crops. Leave the rim a few inches aboveground to keep out water, and cover the top with 18 inches of straw for insulation.

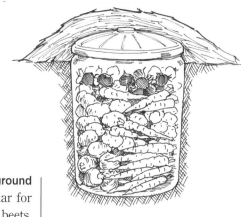

*A trash can makes a good root cellar when sunk into garden soil. Use smaller, shallow cans so you don't have to dig too deep into the soil.*

# Note to Self

**Ron:** Next to duct tape and plastic wrap, those stick 'em notes have to be among the most useful inventions in the history of modern civilization. I'm constantly writing little reminders to myself: "Remove pajamas before getting into shower," "Brush teeth with toothbrush, brush hair with hair brush," "Left shoe on left foot, right shoe on right foot." I don't know how I'd get through the day without those notes.

Stick 'em notes also come in handy now as we rush to finish outdoor gardening chores. The notes are used as reminders for tasks that can be delayed. I put notes on power equipment reminding me to drain the fuel, change the oil, and clean engine parts. There's a note on the tomato stakes that were just removed from the garden. It reads: "Brush soil from stakes, wash stakes with disinfectant, and treat wood with preservative." There are other notes on tools as reminders to brush soil from metal parts, spray the metal with lubricant, and treat wooden handles with warmed linseed oil. The note on my computer says, "Move on to the next chapter."

# 24–25 weeks after average date of last frost

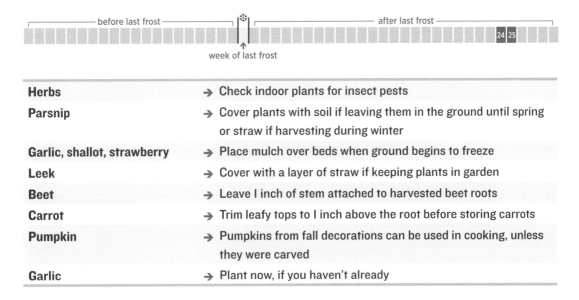

| Herbs | → Check indoor plants for insect pests |
|---|---|
| Parsnip | → Cover plants with soil if leaving them in the ground until spring or straw if harvesting during winter |
| Garlic, shallot, strawberry | → Place mulch over beds when ground begins to freeze |
| Leek | → Cover with a layer of straw if keeping plants in garden |
| Beet | → Leave I inch of stem attached to harvested beet roots |
| Carrot | → Trim leafy tops to I inch above the root before storing carrots |
| Pumpkin | → Pumpkins from fall decorations can be used in cooking, unless they were carved |
| Garlic | → Plant now, if you haven't already |

Save the wood chips and sawdust from wood-cutting projects. However, don't apply wood chips or sawdust directly to the garden. Mix these with grass clippings, manure, or other nitrogen source and allow the mixture to decompose for about a year. This organically rich product can then be added to the garden.

Store pest- and weed-control products. Be sure they're in their original containers with intact labels before storing them under lock and key in a location that will remain above freezing. An unheated garage or garden shed is not a good place to store them.

Store bags or cardboard containers of fertilizer on slatted pallets. Do not allow the fertilizer to come in contact with concrete surfaces because it may absorb moisture from the concrete.

## Seeding and Planting

Plant garlic now, if you didn't get to it several weeks ago. If you don't have straw, it may be helpful to place a floating row cover over the planting. The row cover will warm the soil a little and encourage some root development on the garlic cloves before the ground freezes. We did this a few years ago and then didn't bother with the usual application of straw mulch. The row cover remained in place through the winter. The fact that we didn't apply straw mulch had no effect on the garlic, as the crop we got the following season was as good as ever.

## Maintenance

Check indoor potted herbs for the presence of pests. Some of our plants, especially rosemary and thyme, commonly experience infestations of aphids and mealy bugs. The first sign of aphids is the presence of sticky sap on the leaves. The first sign of mealy bugs is the appearance of powdery or cottony masses of wax on leaves. Applications of insecticidal soap should rid plants of these pests. Just be sure to keep the plants out of direct sunlight for a few days after application of the soap. Read the label for other precautions.

**Throw several inches of soil over parsnips** after a few frosts if you plan to keep them in the ground over winter. Plan to harvest plants early next spring before new shoots start to grow. If you plan to harvest through the winter, cover plants with a 1-foot-deep layer of straw.

**Place mulches over garlic, shallot, and strawberry plantings** when the ground begins to freeze. Mulch keeps the ground from going through freezing–thawing cycles, which can heave garlic or shallot bulbs out of the ground. In the case of strawberries, mulch protects plant crowns from winter injury.

**Cover leeks with a deep layer of straw** if you want to keep them in the garden through winter. As long as soil is not frozen, leeks can be dug as needed.

## Harvest

**Leave 1 inch of stem attached to beet roots** if you are digging beets for winter storage. This extra bit of stem will prevent bleeding of the beet — that is, the release of its red or pink juice.

**Trim the leafy tops from carrots before storing.** Carrots can be stored in the refrigerator for up to a month. For longer storage, place the carrots in a bucket with slightly moist sand and store the bucket in the coldest part of your basement.

**Don't discard pumpkins that were used in Halloween decorations,** unless they were carved up. Store any firm, blemish-free pumpkins and use these to make pies and other hearty autumn dishes. If pumpkins are mushy, remove and save the seeds; then discard the rest of the pumpkin. Roasted pumpkin seeds make a healthy snack.

*Trim the leafy tops from beets before storing, but leave 1 inch of stem attached to the root.*

# SOIL BUILDERS

Treat your soil right, and you will be rewarded with long-lived helpers — earthworms. They can live as long as 8 years and are the primary consumers of organic matter in the soil. In other words, earthworms eat and decompose cornstalks, tomato stems, and other plant debris that is turned under at the end of the growing season.

Of course, what goes in one end must come out the other. Earthworm fecal matter (called castings) is rich in carbon, a product of the decay of plant material. Castings provide a way to keep carbon in garden soil. This carbon is a key building block for fertile soil. Castings also improve soil structure, keeping it loose and crumbly. When castings are numerous, you can assume that the soil is rich and productive. The presence of just a few castings indicate a poor soil. Now, we don't want you running around the neighborhood keeping score of whose garden has the most castings . . .

On second thought, it might encourage better soil management! Increasing the amount of organic matter in soil is the best way to create a better environment for earthworms. Other management techniques to encourage worm populations include watering during dry periods, tilling soil (but not too fine), and using mulches during summer months.

*The castings from earthworms are valuable sources of carbon for improving soil fertility.*

# 26–29 weeks after average date of last frost

| All crops | → Begin planning for next year |
| | → Clean pots and flats for seed starting |
| **Herbs** | → It's not too late to start seed for indoor growing |
| | → Use dishwashing soap and water to clean insects from edibles |
| **Rosemary** | → Keep potting soil moist for healthy plants indoors |

Give thanks for this year's harvest, and then begin planning for next year's vegetable garden. Gather your new seed catalogs and your notes or thoughts on last year's gardens and compile a list of seeds or plants needed for next year's gardens. Though we usually buy seeds and plants locally, we sometimes have to mail-order the hard-to-find varieties. Send mail orders early to ensure availability.

**Check with local gardening organizations and clubs** to see what lectures or courses will be offered this winter. The slow months of winter are a good time to brush up on gardening techniques. And don't overlook the library as a source for exploring new vegetable crops and gardening methods to try. We also find that sharing gardening experiences with friends and neighbors is another way to learn some new tricks.

**Clean pots and flats to be used for starting seeds indoors.** It may seem early, but the seed of some plants can be started soon. For example, we like to start seed of Spanish onions and leeks about 18 weeks before the average last frost date in order to get really huge bulbs by summer harvest. We start slow-to-germinate and slow-to-grow herbs such as parsley 18 to 19 weeks before last frost, too.

## Seeding and Planting

**Sow seeds of culinary herbs** commonly used in your favorite recipes. Pot up the seedlings in 6-inch pots and place the pots on a windowsill that receives direct sunlight through much of the day. Since basil seedlings won't like the cold near windows, these are best grown under fluorescent lights. It would have been better to start these herbs much earlier

in fall, but some may be ready for use by mid-January. These same plants can be planted out in the herb garden next spring, so all is not lost by being late.

## Maintenance

**Do not allow soil of potted rosemary plants to become dry.** Drought is the most common cause of death to this lovely herb when stored indoors through the winter. Also, keep plants at temperatures as cool as you can manage indoors.

**Cleanse insect pests from potted herbs,** using a mild dishwashing soap solution followed by a spray of clear water. Aphids on parsley, mealy bugs on rosemary, and scale on bay are some of the more common pest problems of potted herbs. Always make sure to thoroughly wash and rinse any herbs before cooking with them.

# EXTENDING INTO WINTER

EXTENDING THE HARVEST at this end of the season will take careful planning. For example, start seedlings of crops such as cabbage, collards, and others in the cole family in early to midsummer, depending on your climate. Sow seeds in pots or in a small section of the garden reserved for use as a seedling bed. After 5 to 7 weeks, transplant seedlings from the pots or beds to the garden area where they'll grow on for a fall harvest. Crops such as spinach and lettuce, which do not grow well in the heat of summer, can be planted in late summer for fall and early-winter harvest. The same is true of many other cold-tolerant vegetables, likes carrots, turnips, and radishes.

## GROWING UNDER COVER

Most cold-tolerant vegetables will grow well into winter if grown in cold frames. Greens such as mesclun, mâche (corn salad), spinach, and arugula may be grown in a cold frame for much of the winter, if given a little extra protection in an insulated cold frame.

Extend the harvest of beets, carrots, turnips, parsnips, and rutabaga into winter by placing a deep layer of straw or shredded leaves over the plants just before the ground freezes. To harvest these root vegetables, pull back just enough of the mulch to harvest the amount needed. We've often enjoyed freshly dug carrots at Christmas dinner by using this method of extending the season.

*Even in the coldest regions, some vegetables can be harvested from the garden in winter if protected by a deep layer of straw or shredded leaves.*

# FOOD FOR THOUGHT
# & for Winter

"YOUR EYES ARE bigger than your stomach." Most often expressed in Polish in our family, that's an old saying that provoked many a guilt trip for those of us who piled more food onto our plates than we could eat. The clear implication was that we were being wasteful, a serious offense among generations of folks who had little to spare. Well, we have no problem imposing this same guilt trip on you, but in the context of your vegetable harvest.

Even with a small garden, there are times when the size of the harvest exceeds your capacity to consume it in the few days that the vegetables remain fresh. It just wouldn't be right to waste those vegetables. Feeling guilty yet?

Well, don't. Many of us with large gardens actually *plan* on having a surplus. During the harvest season, our kitchen table is often piled high with fruits and vegetables. There's more than

we need for immediate use, but that is part of our annual gardening plan. Just as with our ancestors, much of what we grow is intended for winter consumption and therefore has to be preserved.

## Putting Food By

There are many methods of preserving vegetables and fruits. These include freezing, canning, drying, and pickling. Over the years we've developed preferences for the method of preserving specific fruits and vegetables. For example, we freeze blueberries, raspberries, strawberries, peppers, peas, cabbage, broccoli, kale, and cauliflower. Initially, we froze green beans, but found them to be rubbery when thawed. Now we can and/or pickle them. Likewise, we think tomatoes tend to lose flavor and texture when frozen, so we can fresh tomatoes. On the other hand, we do freeze roasted and dehydrated tomatoes. In recent years we've taken

to drying certain crops, such as peppers, plum tomatoes, garlic, and herbs.

### Dry Storage

Some vegetables don't need special preservation methods for keeping during winter. We store root crops and potatoes, onions, shallots, garlic, pumpkins, and winter squash without any processing. This method is sometimes referred to as dry storage. With the exception of potatoes, the only requirement is that these vegetables be cured before storing. Curing is done by exposing the harvested crops to warm temperatures for a period of 1 or 2 weeks. Curing promotes healing of any wounds in the surface of vegetables and thickens their skin, which reduces moisture loss during storage. Potatoes don't need curing but those going into storage should not be harvested until they're fully mature. Leeks and root crops such as carrots, turnips, parsnips, and rutabagas can be stored in buckets of sand to preserve their moisture content.

Storage conditions are important in determining how long these crops will keep before they decay or their quality deteriorates. Most vegetables need cold temperatures (above freezing), low humidity, and ventilation during storage. Such conditions were easy to satisfy when people had root cellars, either constructed outdoors into hillsides or indoors, in sections of unheated basements. In modern homes with heated and finished basements, finding an indoor location for cold storage can be difficult. In these situations, the storage life of vegetables kept indoors will be very short — days or weeks, rather than months. A precaution we take with winter squash and pumpkins is to wipe their surfaces with a cloth dampened with

*Many fruits and vegetables can be frozen without any kind of treatment, but some vegetables need to be blanched prior to freezing. If freezing produce in plastic bags, be sure to use only those sold as "freezer bags."*

vinegar, which kills many of the microbes that cause decay.

Requirements for curing and dry storage vary among vegetables. For example, root crops, potatoes, onions, shallots, and garlic keep best at cold temperatures just above freezing. However, pumpkins and winter squash prefer warmer conditions of 50 to 60°F (10 to 15°C).

*Dry storage is an inexpensive way to keep root crops, onions and their relatives, and winter squash.*

### Freezing the Harvest

For the vast majority of vegetables, freezing is the most popular method of preserving crops for winter consumption. In many cases the only preparation is to slice or chop the vegetable and toss the pieces into a freezer bag or other plastic container. We do this with onions, peppers, rhubarb, and strawberries. If using plastic bags, be sure to buy those labeled as freezer bags. The plastic is a little thicker than ordinary storage bags. Thicker plastic reduces the risk of the stored food becoming dehydrated or oxidized, a condition known as freezer burn.

Most vegetables need to be blanched before they are frozen. Blanching is done by dropping vegetables into boiling water or by steaming for a few minutes. The purpose is to eliminate or slow the action of certain enzymes that cause loss of color, flavor, and other qualities of the frozen food. The precise time for blanching varies with the vegetable. Since we can never remember specific blanching times, we keep a book on food preservation handy for quick reference (see Resources, page 185, for suggestions).

## Canning the Goods

There are certain vegetables that taste better when canned rather than frozen. That's one reason why we do a lot of canning. Also, we can always find shelf space for canned goods, but freezer space is limited and fills up quickly. However, canning requires more equipment, more time, and more attention to detail than does freezing.

Equipment needs for canning include jars, lids and rings (or screw bands), sturdy tongs for lifting jars, a spatula, a canning funnel, and, of course, a canner. Most of the time we use a boiling-water canner, but many experts recommend using only a pressure canner, as it reduces the risk of botulism. It would be wise for anyone just learning to can vegetables to use the pressure canner.

The risk of food contamination and spoilage is greater with canned goods than frozen ones. To eliminate this risk, pay careful attention to proper handling procedures for vegetables, sterilization of canning jars and lids, and the required processing temperature and time for each vegetable. Canning is one of those techniques best learned by working with someone who has had considerable experience and has survived to share that know-how with you. With increasing interest in home food preservation, many organizations offer courses and hands-on workshops on canning.

*Herbs are especially well suited to air-drying. Simply hang small bunches in a dark but airy location.*

## Drying

The oldest method of food preservation is dehydration. Our ancestors spread food items in the sun, sometimes after heavy salting, and let them dry. While we have abandoned our animal-skin duds for cotton and polyester attire, we still employ some simple methods for drying food items, especially herbs and hot peppers. For example, we snip shoots of oregano, thyme, and sage, tie them into small bunches, and hang them in a warm, airy location for drying. We also thread chili peppers together and hang these up to dry.

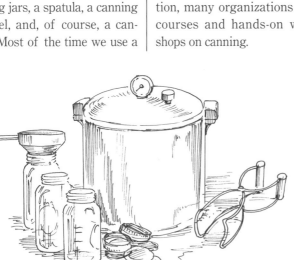

*Canning fruits and vegetables requires more equipment than other preservation methods do, as well as more attention to detail, since there is a risk of food contamination if canning is done improperly.*

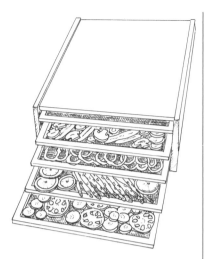

*Dehydrators make the drying of vegetables an easy task.*

**Electric dehydrators.** Most food dehydration today is done with an electric dehydrator. These devices typically consist of a stack of drying trays, an electric heat source, and, preferably, a fan to circulate air. The price range of dehydrators varies from Yugo to Mercedes depending upon the construction materials, capacity, and such accessories as thermostats and timers. We opted for the Chevy or Toyota level of expense. Our dehydrator is made of durable plastic, and it has a variable thermostat for temperature control and a fan to ensure even distribution of heat. Since many variables determine the amount of time required to complete the drying process, we elected not to go with higher-priced models with timers. It may not be as high-tech, but we prefer to look at the clock on the wall and to periodically examine the condition of vegetables in the dehydrator to determine when they have dried to the proper degree.

**Drying in the oven.** A commercial dehydrator is a nice item to have, but anyone with a kitchen oven can dry vegetables. Care has to be taken to keep oven temperatures low (200°F [93°C] or lower) to avoid cooking the vegetable, and unless you keep the oven door open, air circulation is a problem. All in all, oven drying is not a very efficient way to dry vegetables, but if that's what you have, go with it.

**Timing.** Though there are guidelines for time required to dry specific vegetables, getting the timing right is often a matter of trial and error. Factors such as size, thickness, and natural moisture content of the vegetable, as well as relative humidity, can influence drying time. Generally, when vegetables are pliable like leather but with no obvious evidence of moisture, they are done. As a simple test for presence of moisture, tear a sample of the food item in half and squeeze a piece to see if any water oozes out. If it does, continue the dehydration process.

We let a few vegetables dry beyond the leathery stage. Herbs, hot peppers, and garlic are dried to the crisp stage. Many of these will eventually be ground up in a food processor or spice grinder prior to use.

**Storage.** The key to storing dehydrated vegetables is to put them in airtight containers, so they're protected from moisture. Our favorite storage container is the

*Two tablespoons of rice wrapped in facial tissue and placed in an airtight jar of dehydrated vegetables will absorb any moisture that is in the container.*

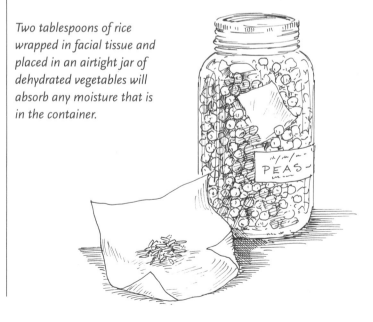

canning jar. As an extra precaution against moisture absorption, you can put a packet of silica gel in the bottom of the jar. The gel is a desiccant and will absorb any moisture in the jar. Since we don't keep a supply of silica gel packets on hand, we make our own packets of desiccant by wrapping 2 tablespoons of rice in a few sheets of facial tissue. Remember when Grandma put rice grains in the salt shaker to keep the salt from caking due to moisture absorption? It works! We've also used powdered milk instead of rice as a desiccant.

## Pickling

The final method of food preservation we want to bring to your attention is pickling. Pickling starts with a mixture of water, vinegar, and salt, which is brought to a boil. This is the basic brine for pickling. From that point on, there are as many recipes for pickling as there are picklers. For beginners who find themselves in a pickle, keep it simple. Select fresh, crisp, and clean vegetables — whether they're cucumbers, green beans, white onions, or combinations of vegetables — and pack these into canning jars. Then add items to enhance the flavor. These might be dill sprigs, shoots of rosemary,

garlic cloves, peppercorns, or a spoonful of pickling spices. Pour the boiling salt-vinegar-water solution over the vegetable(s) and seal the jars; store in the refrigerator. If the pickled vegetables are not going to be used within a few weeks, it will be necessary to process the jars in a boiling-water bath or pressure canner.

Most of the preservation methods mentioned will keep vegetables preserved for a year or longer. However, after a year, the quality of the food item does decline. It's a good idea to write the date when each item was canned, frozen, or dried. We keep records of what and how much of each item we preserve. This gives us an idea of how much we consume annually and how much we need to preserve each year.

Yes, all of these efforts are time consuming, but the rewards come in winter, in the form of a secure feeling, knowing that we have our homegrown fruits and vegetables to sustain us.

*Pickling is a time-honored method of preserving vegetables. It begins with a hot solution of water, vinegar, and salt poured over vegetables in glass containers.*

# Resources

## INTERNET RESOURCES

**Biological Control: A Guide to Natural Enemies in North America**
Cornell University, New York
State Agricultural Experiment Station
*www.nysaes.cornell.edu/ent/biocontrol*
Information and pictures of beneficial insects

**Garden Writers Association**
*www.gardenwriters.org*
Information on the Plant a Row for the Hungry program

**Gardening Resources**
Cornell University, Department of Horticulture
*www.hort.cornell.edu/gardening*
General gardening information and tips on growing specific vegetables

**Green Tomato Recipes**
Group Recipes
*www.grouprecipes.com/green-tomato*

**Heat-Related Illnesses**
*www.aafp.org/afp/980901ap/barrow.html*
First published by Michael W. Barrow and Katherine A. Clark in the September 1, 1998, edition of *American Family Physician,* for the American Academy of Family Physicians

**International Seed Saving Institute**
*www.seedsave.org*
Fact sheets about seed saving and vegetables whose seeds are easy to save

**National Center for Home Food Preservation**
University of Georgia
*www.uga.edu/nchfp*
A complete source of information about food preservation

**National Climatic Data Center**
National Oceanic and Atmospheric Administration
*www.ncdc.noaa.gov/oa/ncdc.html*
"The world's largest archive of climate data" including average frost dates around the country and worldwide climate information

**National Institute of Food and Agriculture**
United States Department of Agriculture
*www.csrees.usda.gov*
Lots of great information and a map to help you find your local cooperative extension office

**Ohioline: Yard & Garden**
College of Food, Agricultural, and Environmental Sciences
*http://ohioline.osu.edu/lines/hygs.html*

General gardening information and tips on growing specific vegetables

**Saving Vegetable Seeds: Tomatoes, Peppers, Peas and Beans**
University of Minnesota Extension
*www.extension.umn.edu/distribution/horticulture/M1226.html*
Online edition of a 2008 article by Jill MacKensie on vegetables whose seeds are easy to save

**Sustainable Agriculture Research and Education**
*www.sare.org*
Information and publications on sustainable agriculture, including cover crops

**Vegetable IPM**
Texas A&M University
*http://vegipm.tamu.edu*
"Dedicated to Integrated Pest Management for the home vegetable garden" with excellent garden pest photographs

**What's Wrong with My Plant?**
University of Minnesota Extension
*www.extension.umn.edu/gardeninfo/diagnostics/vegetable*
A great resource to help you identify vegetable plant diseases

## GARDENING SUPPLIES

### Vegetable Seed Sources

Harris Seeds
800-544-7938
www.harrisseeds.com

Johnny's Selected Seed
877-564-6697
www.johnnyseeds.com

Jung Quality Garden Seeds
800-297-3123
www.jungseed.com

Park Seed Co.
800-213-0076
www.parkseed.com

Peaceful Valley Farm &
    Garden Supply
888-784-1722
www.groworganic.com

Pinetree Garden Seeds
207-926-3400
www.superseeds.com

Territorial Seed Company
800-626-0866
www.territorialseed.com

Totally Tomatoes
800-345-5977
www.totallytomato.com

Vermont Bean Seed Company
800-349-1071
www.vermontbean.com

W. Atlee Burpee & Co.
800-333-5808
www.burpee.com

### General Supplies and Tools

A. M. Leonard
800-543-8955
www.amleo.com

CobraHead LLC
866-962-6272
www.cobrahead.com

Gardener's Supply Company
888-833-1412
www.gardeners.com

Peaceful Valley Farm & Garden
    Supply
888-784-1722
www.groworganic.com

### Reflective Mulch

Gardener's Supply Company
888-833-1412
www.gardeners.com

Totally Tomatoes
800-345-5977
www.totallytomato.com

Territorial Seed Company
800-626-0866
www.territorialseed.com

## BOOKS

### Other Gardening References We Like

*Building Soils for Better Crops*, 2nd edition, by Fred Magdoff and Harold
    van Es. 2000. Sustainable Agriculture Network, Beltsville, MD.
*Crockett's Victory Garden* by James Underwood Crockett. 1977. Little,
    Brown & Company, Boston.
*Dick Raymond's Gardening Year* by Dick Raymond. 1985. Linden Press/
    Simon & Schuster, New York.
*Vegetable Growing Handbook*, 3rd edition, by Walter E. Splittstoesser. 1990.
    Van Nostrand Reinhold, New York.

### Pest Management References

*The Gardener's Guide to Common-Sense Pest Control* by William
    Olkowski, Sheila Daar, and Helga Olkowski. 1995. Taunton Press,
    Newtown, CT.
*Insect, Disease & Weed I.D. Guide,* edited by Jill Jesiolowski Cebenko and
    Deborah L. Martin. 2001. Rodale, Emmaus, PA.
*The Organic Gardener's Handbook of Natural Insect and Disease Control,*
    edited by Barbara W. Ellis and Fern Marshall Bradley. 1996. Rodale,
    Emmaus, PA.

### Using and Preserving Garden Produce

*Garden Way's Joy of Gardening Cookbook* by Janet Ballantyne. 1984.
    Garden Way, Troy, NY.
*Keeping the Harvest* by Nancy Chioffi and Gretchen Mead. 2002. Storey
    Publishing, North Adams, MA.
*Serving Up the Harvest* by Andrea Chesman. 2007. Storey Publishing,
    North Adams, MA.
*Vegetables Every Day* by Jack Bishop. 2001. HarperCollins, New York.

# Average Frost-Free Date for Selected Locations
## (Source: National Climatic Data Center)

The table below is an excerpt from the National Climatic Data Center's Freeze/Frost Probability tables. We've included the average date of last frost for selected cities in each state, with the exception of Hawaii. This information will be useful to many who garden near these locations. However, keep in mind that local site factors as discussed in the section "Garden Planning Week by Week" (page 22) will influence the average date of last frost where you live. Also realize that the dates given are averages. That means there is still a 50 percent chance of frost after the average date. We recommend waiting about 2 weeks after the average date to set out tender or warm-season crops such as tomatoes and peppers.

| State and City | Average Date of Last Frost (32°F, 0°C) | State and City | Average Date of Last Frost (32°F, 0°C) |
|---|---|---|---|
| **ALABAMA** | | **COLORADO** | |
| Birmingham | Apr 2 | Colorado Springs | May 4 |
| Huntsville | Mar 30 | Denver | Apr 30 |
| Mobile | Feb 28 | Fort Collins | May 4 |
| **ALASKA** | | **CONNECTICUT** | |
| Anchorage | May 8 | Bridgeport | Apr 11 |
| Fairbanks | May 15 | Danbury | May 1 |
| Nome | Jun 11 | Hartford | Apr 26 |
| **ARIZONA** | | **DELAWARE** | |
| Flagstaff | Jun 9 | Dover | Apr 8 |
| Phoenix | Dec 16 | Newark | Apr 18 |
| Tucson | Jan 19 | Wilmington | Apr 10 |
| **ARKANSAS** | | **FLORIDA** | |
| El Dorado | Mar 28 | Jacksonville | Feb 26 |
| Fayetteville | Apr 10 | Pensacola | Feb 22 |
| Little Rock | Mar 22 | Tallahassee | Mar 22 |
| **CALIFORNIA** | | **GEORGIA** | |
| Fresno | Feb 4 | Albany | Mar 17 |
| Gilroy | Feb 17 | Atlanta | Mar 24 |
| Sacramento | Feb 10 | Savannah | Mar 1 |
| | | **HAWAII N/A** | |

# Average Frost-Free Date for Selected Locations *(continued)*
## (Source: National Climatic Data Center)

| State and City | Average Date of Last Frost (32°F, 0°C) | State and City | Average Date of Last Frost (32°F, 0°C) |
|---|---|---|---|
| **IDAHO** | | **MAINE** | |
| Boise | May 10 | Bangor | May 6 |
| Lewiston | Apr 12 | Portland | May 2 |
| Pocatello | May 23 | Presque Isle | May 21 |
| **ILLINOIS** | | **MARYLAND** | |
| Carbondale | Apr 15 | Baltimore | Apr 11 |
| Chicago | Apr 25 | Frederick | Apr 9 |
| Peoria | Apr 19 | Savage River | May 4 |
| **INDIANA** | | **MASSACHUSETTS** | |
| Evansville | Apr 10 | Amherst | May 10 |
| Indianapolis | Apr 17 | Boston | Apr 7 |
| South Bend | Apr 26 | East Wareham | Apr 25 |
| **IOWA** | | **MICHIGAN** | |
| Cedar Rapids | Apr 22 | Detroit | Apr 26 |
| Des Moines | Apr 20 | Grand Rapids | May 5 |
| Mason City | May 1 | Grayling | Jun 4 |
| **KANSAS** | | **MINNESOTA** | |
| Salina | Apr 15 | Duluth | May 21 |
| Topeka | Apr 19 | Minneapolis | Apr 30 |
| Wichita | Apr 12 | Rochester | May 3 |
| **KENTUCKY** | | **MISSISSIPPI** | |
| Lexington | Apr 15 | Biloxi | Feb 23 |
| Louisville | Apr 8 | Jackson | Mar 23 |
| Madisonville | Apr 12 | Tupelo | Apr 5 |
| **LOUISIANA** | | **MISSOURI** | |
| Alexandria | Feb 27 | Kansas City | Apr 7 |
| New Orleans | Feb 12 | Saint Louis | Apr 7 |
| Shreveport | Mar 10 | Springfield | Apr 15 |

| State and City | Average Date of Last Frost (32°F, 0°C) | State and City | Average Date of Last Frost (32°F, 0°C) |
|---|---|---|---|
| **MONTANA** | | **NORTH CAROLINA** | |
| Billings | May 4 | Asheville | Apr 12 |
| Great Falls | May 17 | Charlotte | Mar 29 |
| Helena | May 19 | Wilmington | Apr 2 |
| **NEBRASKA** | | **NORTH DAKOTA** | |
| Grand Island | Apr 26 | Bismarck | May 14 |
| Omaha | Apr 25 | Fargo | May 10 |
| Scotts Bluff | May 3 | Minot | May 12 |
| **NEVADA** | | **OHIO** | |
| Elko | Jun 9 | Cincinnati | Apr 13 |
| Las Vegas | Feb 16 | Cleveland | Apr 30 |
| Reno | May 21 | Columbus | Apr 24 |
| **NEW HAMPSHIRE** | | **OKLAHOMA** | |
| Berlin | May 20 | Enid | Apr 4 |
| Durham | May 13 | Oklahoma City | Apr 1 |
| Nashua | May 7 | Tulsa | Mar 27 |
| **NEW JERSEY** | | **OREGON** | |
| Atlantic City | Apr 24 | Baker | Jun 3 |
| Newark | Apr 3 | Eugene | Apr 22 |
| Sussex | May 9 | Portland | Mar 23 |
| **NEW MEXICO** | | **PENNSYLVANIA** | |
| Albuquerque | Apr 16 | Philadelphia | Apr 6 |
| Carlsbad | Mar 31 | Pittsburgh | Apr 29 |
| El Rito | May 25 | State College | Apr 27 |
| **NEW YORK** | | **RHODE ISLAND** | |
| Albany | May 2 | Kingston | May 8 |
| Buffalo | Apr 24 | Newport | Apr 20 |
| New York City: Central Park | Apr 1 | Providence | Apr 16 |

# Average Frost-Free Date for Selected Locations (continued)
## (Source: National Climatic Data Center)

| State and City | Average Date of Last Frost (32°F, 0°C) | State and City | Average Date of Last Frost (32°F, 0°C) |
|---|---|---|---|
| **SOUTH CAROLINA** | | **VIRGINIA** | |
| Charleston | Mar 9 | Charlottesville | Apr 7 |
| Columbia | Apr 1 | Norfolk | Mar 20 |
| Greenville | Apr 4 | Richmond | Apr 6 |
| **SOUTH DAKOTA** | | **WASHINGTON** | |
| Aberdeen | May 8 | Kennewick | Apr 8 |
| Rapid City | May 9 | Seattle | Mar 10 |
| Sioux Falls | May 3 | Spokane | May 2 |
| **TENNESSEE** | | **WEST VIRGINIA** | |
| Knoxville | Apr 16 | Beckley | May 3 |
| Memphis | Mar 22 | Charleston | Apr 22 |
| Nashville | Apr 6 | Morgantown | Apr 30 |
| **TEXAS** | | **WISCONSIN** | |
| Corpus Christi | Feb 3 | Eau Claire | May 7 |
| Dallas | Mar 3 | Green Bay | May 6 |
| El Paso | Mar 22 | Milwaukee | Apr 25 |
| **UTAH** | | **WYOMING** | |
| Cedar City | May 21 | Casper | May 22 |
| Saint George | Mar 20 | Cheyenne | May 12 |
| Salt Lake City | Apr 19 | Sheridan | May 28 |
| **VERMONT** | | | |
| Burlington | May 8 | | |
| Montpelier | May 11 | | |
| Saint Johnsbury | May 19 | | |

| DATE | NOTES |
| --- | --- |
| | |

| DATE | NOTES |
|------|-------|
|      |       |

# Index

Page numbers in *italics* indicate illustrations.
Page numbers in **bold** indicate charts.

seeds *(continued)*

# Other Storey Titles You Will Enjoy

*The Beginner's Guide to Preserving Food at Home,* by Janet Chadwick.
The best and quickest methods for preserving every common vegetable and fruit,
with easy instructions to encourage even first-timers.
240 pages. Paper. ISBN 978-1-60342-145-4.

*The Complete Compost Gardening Guide,* by Barbara Pleasant
& Deborah L. Martin.
Everything a gardener needs to know to produce the best compost, nourishment
for abundant, flavorful vegetables.
320 pages. Paper. ISBN 978-1-58017-702-3.

*The Gardener's A–Z Guide to Growing Organic Food,*
by Tanya L. K. Denckla.
An invaluable resource for growing, harvesting, and storing 765 varieties
of vegetables, fruits, herbs, and nuts.
496 pages. Paper. ISBN 978-1-58017-370-4.

*Starter Vegetable Gardens,* by Barbara Pleasant.
A great resource for beginning vegetable gardeners: 24 no-fail plans for small
organic gardens.
180 pages. Paper. ISBN 978-1-60342-529-2.
Hardcover. ISBN 978-1-60342-530-8.

*The Vegetable Gardener's Bible,* **2nd edition,** by Edward C. Smith.
The 10th Anniversary Edition of the vegetable gardening classic, with expanded
coverage of additional vegetables, fruits, and herbs.
352 pages. Paper. ISBN 978-1-60342-475-2. Hardcover. ISBN 978-1-60342-476-9.

*The Veggie Gardener's Answer Book,* by Barbara W. Ellis.
Insider's tips and tricks, practical advice, and organic wisdom for vegetable
growers everywhere.
432 pages. Flexibind. ISBN 978-1-60342-024-2.

These and other books from Storey Publishing are available
wherever quality books are sold or by calling 1-800-441-5700.
Visit us at *www.storey.com.*